What is being said about this

A marvelous book! It honestly reflects failures and disappointments...but is filled with hope, encouragement, and positive action steps towards accomplishing hope-filled lives.

The take-home message is that we can still receive, and still give, JOY, no matter our circumstances. It takes fortitude and effort to re-focus our thinking...but the struggle is worth the results!!

The hope and the inspiring message: I am who I am because Jesus loves me! Period.

Diana Waggoner, Executive Director
Kim Foundation

A book born out of personal tragedy to triumph in Christ. Brad takes those wanting more than just surviving their mental health issues, to freedom and real transformation. A practical hands-on approach from start to finish. Brad takes those willing to do the hard work of recovery step by step on a life changing journey in becoming what they have only dreamed about.

Allen Lee Minnig
LMHP, CP

A sense of excitement is building inside me to finally have a workbook to use with our Fresh Hope group. The organization, readability, and content are right on! I now understand better why people get stuck in a mindset. What an inspiration to all of us!

Jamie
Leader of FH in Lincoln

What is being said about Fresh Hope...

One of the great challenges for people living with mental illness is finding a spiritual community that will provide encouragement and inclusion. Fresh Hope provides congregations with a model for positive, hopeful living. The program invites people diagnosed with mental illness and their families to understand the illness and see beyond it to a full life. Both facilitators and participants sing the praises of this program, declaring that it has moved them from hopelessness to joy."

Rev. Sally Carlson
Hospital Chaplain with 10 years of providing spiritual support in mental health care facilities

Fresh Hope

Brad Hoefs

www.xulonpress.com

Table of Contents

Acknowledgements

Advent: December 6, 2012

It was seventeen years ago, at this very time of the year, that a group of God's people surrounded my family and me, and began to provide us a safe place for healing. In December of 1995, we were in such emotional pain that we could not even find it within our beings to put up our Christmas tree. So, two ladies came to our home and decorated it. It was this kind of Christian love that this group of people began to shower upon us. Never before had we experienced God's grace (Jesus with skin on) so powerfully.

This small group, made up of all kinds of people, was the founder of the church that I continue to pastor today, Community of Grace. They started a church with the purpose of it being a safe place for our family to heal following what had been six months of "living hell." As we were experiencing "living hell" these folks came and walked through it with us. They ministered to us as though they were ministering angels from the Lord. And little did I know at that time that my journey to discovering fresh hope had begun.

A quote by Walter Winchell describes this perfectly, "True friends are those who walk in when the rest of the world has walked out on you." These folks walked into our lives when it felt like so many had walked out. And through them, and because of them, God gave us a community of His grace. And we began to heal. I dedicate this book to that group of people. Because of their understanding of God's grace and mercy, we are whole and healthy people today. Had they not come along side us, held us, and sometimes carried us, I do not know where we would be today. It is sad to say, but seldom do people experience the grace of God as did we so powerfully through the body of Christ.

Besides the folks who came along side us, there is one person who stayed with me when many others would have walked out. That person is Donna. She is the most incredible person I know. She has shown grace, forgiveness, understanding, mercy, hope, character, strength, and a deep, deep love of God like no other human being I have ever known. And I am a very blessed man to have her as my wife. She has been and is my wellness coach! Without her, I would not be where I am today. I thank the Lord for her every day. When I "grow up" I want to be just like her. She has an inner strength and a depth of character that comes from the Lord which amazes me. I didn't think I could love her more than the day I married her, but I do. From the depths of my heart I praise God for her and I thank her for being the woman of God she has been and continues to be today. She takes her vow of "for better-for worse" seriously. For this, I am ever so grateful! I dedicate this book to the love of my life, who has been and continues to be filled with the Lord's fresh hope.

I also want to dedicate this book to my children, Noah and Noelle. They have experienced the trauma of having a Dad whose untreated mental illness brought about the implosion of their world. They have experienced the best and the worst of what the Christian church has to offer. They have experienced so much pain and hurt that was been inflicted by not only the results of their Father's undiagnosed and untreated disorder, but also from fellow believers. And yet, they still trust Jesus. And tears fill my eyes as I write this, for I am so grateful for them. They too have been on this journey, not by choice, but out of love. And they have shown the same grace and strength of character as their Mom. We are so proud of them. They are happy, whole, and healthy married adults who love the Lord.

Also, I want to dedicate this book to my extended family: Mom and Dad, Tom and Brenda. You all have been there for us "no matter what"! Thank you for your love, care, concern, prayers, and ongoing support. And to my brothers-in-law and your families, I am grateful for your prayers. I thank the Lord for you all!

This book is also dedicated to those who have been and are part of the original Fresh Hope group on Tuesday nights. You guys are the best! You have been a great inspiration to me. And I have never seen lives change so easily as in this peer-to-peer support group called Fresh Hope. My heart is overwhelmed with thankfulness when I see what the Lord is doing in your lives.

And finally I want to dedicate this book to the two people in my life that have not had to experience the pain of untreated mental illness: Jayden and Ava. You two grandchildren are the joy of Grandma's and my lives. My heart explodes with love for the two of you! You two are the "icing on the cake" in regards to God's second chance and new beginnings in my life. On the days when recovery is difficult, you are Papa's motivation to stay well.

Writing this has been a team effort:

- Sincere thanks to Patty Carr, Chris Gryzen, and Mandy Vitense, who helped me get the first few chapters "going" and encouraged me to continue writing. Without your help, I probably still would only be thinking about writing the book.

- Grateful appreciation to the ministry staff (especially my wife, Donna, and Susan Hager) and to the members of Community of Grace, who allowed me to devote the time to focus on this project.

- And a very special thank you to the kind of friend that is like family, Julie Koenemann. Without her this project would not have finally been completed. Because of you coming along side of me and finalizing the manuscript, with hours and hours of proofreading and editing, this project could finally "go to print." Julie, you're the best! Thank you!

- A very heartfelt thank you to my peer accountability group: Pastor Jim McGaffin, Pastor Randy Fontaine, and Pastor Lindley Jacobson. For the last 10 years you have held me accountable for my emotional and spiritual health. You have "been there" for me without fail. You've encouraged me, held me up, and given me a gentle push when necessary. Thank you! As Pastor Jim always says, "When the dust settles, we will all be standing." Thanks for continuing to hang in there with me during my "dirty dustbowl" days!

- To everyone who inspired, motivated, encouraged, and prayed for me through this process, a list too abundant to name (and I wouldn't want to forget anyone), my sincere gratitude. You know who you are, and more importantly, so does God.

- And finally, a very grateful thanks to Dr. Michael Egger. Without your encouragement to start Fresh Hope I would never had done it. You patiently and persistently encouraged me to move forward with it. And when I asked for you to come along side Fresh Hope and help, you quickly said "Yes." Thank you for your help and insights. I am blessed to have you as my doctor for the past 17 years. The Lord knew I would need a man of faith as my doctor who could help me on my journey to wholeness and hope. Thank you!

Foreword

As a professional mental health therapist, I am always looking for first-rate material I can utilize to help my clients suffering from a plethora of mental health disorders. For those suffering from mood disorders I have found Brad Hoefs' book, *"Fresh Hope"* riveting. Not written from a point of view that merely theorizes what mental health is, but this book is born from real world experiences with truth that works. Brad takes the reader on a spiritual journey to wholeness, transcending the murky waters of mood disorders toward health and well-being.

Brad's story is real. I know, because I have met Brad and heard his story, and with great affection say, "He is my pastor." Like Brad, from tragedy to triumph, like the mythic Phoenix reborn from fire and ash to a new life, so you, too, can be reborn to a new life, one of mental stability and renewal step by step.

No matter where you have been, what you have been through, whether you are in the throes of despair and hopelessness, just surviving or feeling stable for the moment…there is more… so much more.

With clarity, and lovingly written, the reader is able to see the fingerprints of God woven on every page of this eye-opening book. Why allow the hidden monster within to continue to devastate, create chaos, and dictate the course of your life? Reclaim your life and allow God to redeem your suffering. Encouraging, explicit, resounding in truth…begin your own journey and allow God to redeem your pain and suffering into trophies of His wonderful grace.

Fresh hope is a must-read for friends, pastors, wives, husbands, and family members seeking to better understand their loved one's suffering from a mood disorder.

Take a risk. You have nothing to lose except you sanity, and everything to gain. Begin your journey and you will find God lighting your path into <u>Fresh Hope</u>, and the freedom to live life as you always dreamed about.

Allen L. Minnig
LMHP, C.P., Omaha, NE, 2012

(Don't Skip This — Please Read First!)

PREFACE

An Introduction to Fresh Hope

T oo often mental health "recovery" focuses on learning to cope and survive with your mental illness; which leads to a helplessness, hopelessness, and a sense of permanent loss. Persistent mental health challenges easily destroy one's self-confidence and rob you of the joy of living. I know, because I've been there.

In 2001, I experienced yet another very public and humiliating manic episode. I thought I was coping and "dealing with" my disorder. But, I got my medicines messed up one night, double taking one of them. So the next night I just didn't take my mood stabilizer, which led to approximately three weeks of insanity and crazy behavior; most of which I don't remember. Here I was seven years following my diagnosis, only to repeat almost exactly what had happened years earlier.

You see, seven years earlier I had a manic episode that became public and ever so painful to so many. My actions hurt my wife and family deeply, along with a church full of members. After months of news reports in the paper and on TV, and three months of a living hell that took me to the brink of suicide, I ended up in a hospital in Michigan where I received a name for this "monster" within me that I had tried so hard to control.

For the first seven years following my diagnosis I was on a journey. But it really wasn't a journey towards wholeness, but rather what I call a "journey of coping."

Somehow I had mistakenly come to think that what I needed to do was figure out how to "cope" with having a mental health disorder. No one talked to me about wellness verses coping. No one ever told me that I could have a rich and full life *in spite* of this disorder. So for the first seven years of my recovery, I was simply coping and trying to learn how to "live with" my disorder; and I'll be darned if the disorder snuck up behind me only to bring me to this point of relapse.

Following my relapse in 2001, a friend told me he now knew that I really had a mental illness. He said he knew me to be a smart person, smart enough to not repeat what had happened in 1995. Thus my relapse and repeated manic episode was confirmation to him that it was real. For me, it was confirmation that I wanted my life back! I wanted to live again – in spite of my disorder. I knew I wanted more out of my life than just coping with my illness. So, for the first time I began to attend a mental health support group, believing I would find people there who had found the "key" to living a rich and full life in spite of their mental health issues. But to my dismay, I found a group of people struggling, pretty hopeless, and beat down by their illnesses. And after each meeting I attended, I found myself discouraged, sad, powerless, and thinking, "There has got to be more to my life than just allowing the management of daily coping of my disorder to take over my whole life." And it is this frustration that led me to my journey to fresh hope: fresh hope that is found in the Lord, fresh hope that empowers me to live a full and rich life *in spite* of my disorder, fresh hope that enables me to live symptom-free of my disorder as I proactively live out my wellness plan.

Hi, my name is Brad and I have bipolar disorder. And like you, there's so much more to me than an unwanted mental health diagnosis. I am a loving husband to the strongest, most loving wife a man could ever ask for, a father to great adult children and a papa to two of the most wonderful grandchildren in the world. I'm a creative, intuitive person with solid leadership skills. I am a musician and artist. I am a follower of Jesus and I am a pastor. I have what some call a mental illness. It *is* part of me, but it is not ALL of me. However, I am not my diagnosis. And I will NOT allow others to minimize me to a diagnosis or marginalize me because of the label of bipolar. I didn't ask for it. I didn't seek it out. It's not a character flaw nor is it a moral issue. And it's not a spiritual/faith issue! I can choose to let it define me, confine me, refine me, outshine me, or I can choose to move on and leave it behind me.

Today, it's a small part of my life. Yet I know all too well that bipolar disorder or any mental health issue left untreated can easily destroy your entire life! I know that because prior to 1995 this disorder was beginning to destroy every part of my life. But today, I have fresh hope!

What is Fresh Hope?

Fresh Hope is a journey to wholeness in one's life after a mental health diagnosis.

Fresh Hope is learning to live a FULL and rich life in spite of a mental health diagnosis.

Fresh Hope is empowerment to take my life back.

Fresh Hope is the process which enables me to "rule over" my disorder, as opposed to coping with it.

Fresh Hope comes from the Lord!

During the seven years following my relapse I began to study, search, and pray for ways that would bring back a joy to living. Knowing that the Lord was key to finding that joy, I searched high and low to find a support group that was faith-based. I found nothing. I searched on Google for nearly two years looking for websites where I might find materials for starting a faith-based support group. I found nothing.

As I talked with my doctor, Dr. Michael Egger, about this, he asked, "Have you ever thought about starting a support group based upon your own personal journey"? I brushed it off and thought, "Yeah, sure. When people find out that I'm a pastor who made the newspaper and was on the news and went through all these things, they'll stop coming immediately." And yet, I couldn't let go of his challenge. It was as though the Lord was saying to me, "This is the way that I plan to redeem all of the past years of pain and struggle." But I kept tripping over my past and myself, and I assumed others would trip over it, too. So I put off the thought of starting anything at all. Yet I could not get the idea out of my head of a group that was safe, where people could experience hope, healing, and unconditional grace. And from fourteen years of recovery – the first seven only a "coping recovery", and the second seven years a recovery based upon wellness– Fresh Hope was born.

We held our first meeting of Fresh Hope on Tuesday, February 3, 2010. We started with 17 people the first night. In the weeks that followed the group got smaller. But during that time we all began to learn the narratives of one another's lives. And through this process Fresh Hope began to blossom and evolve into what is now a network of groups that are beginning to spring up in various locales throughout the country.

Starting Fresh Hope has brought more healing and more hope into my life than I could have ever imagined. I marvel at how the smallest little thing that somebody says gives huge breakthrough to another person on the exact night they need to hear it. In all my years of ministry as a pastor, I have never seen lives change so easily.

What makes Fresh Hope different from other support groups for people with mental health issues?

Fresh Hope is faith-based and Christ-centered. We don't apologize for it. We look at our mood disorder as we do with all things: through the lens of faith, faith in a God Who is the God of the universe; Who created us, made us, and is all powerful and all-knowing; the true God; the God of the Scriptures, Father, Son and Holy Spirit; the Father Who loved us so much that He sent His only son, Jesus Christ, to die for us. And we don't apologize for it.

With that said, understand that we don't get hyper-spiritual in our Fresh Hope meetings, either. People are where they are, and we're fine with that. I've seen many people who have little to no faith, no faith at all, or may even have a different faith, come and be quite comfortable, because more than anything, it's a safe place. It's a safe place to experience God's love and not have the Bible shoved down your throat or somebody coming at you.

When people speak from their own experience, it's hard to argue with them, especially when somebody says, "This is how I've experienced the Lord in my recovery." But the purpose of the group is not to be a Bible study, nor is it supposed to be a debate about spiritual matters. Instead it is a group that is there to help extend hope, where hope is extended from a Christian perspective to those who have mood disorders, hope that God is able and quite capable and will do something great.

Our groups are peer facilitator-led, versus group-led or led by an outside facilitator. Our leaders are trained to give some direction to the group, not in a therapeutic way, not as a therapist would lead a support group, but different than just letting the group take its own direction. There are topics and a specific plan to follow, especially for the first half of the meeting time.

Our tenets are based on a model of faith-filled wellness. You might call it faith-filled recovery principles. Our bias is that one can manage his or her own recovery and live a fulfilling and joy-filled life. Now when I say manage one's own recovery, it means that you're the lead active person in it. You're the person taking active responsibility for your recovery, with your doctor assisting and helping, but you are pushing through and choosing to live.

We recognize that even when we're sick, we still have the power to choose. We believe that faith enables us to continue to operate. And sometimes faith is all that we have when we are at our sickest.

We recognize the difference between our brain and our mind and our soul. Our brain is the organ and our mind is what the brain does. The Lord uses our minds to feed our souls through His Word; our faith is part of our soul. This distinction is fundamentally important. It is because of the distinction between our brain, mind, and soul that we would maintain that at times our brains are not chemically balanced; causing the function of the brain to bring about unhealthy/unbalanced thinking and actions. These unhealthy thoughts and actions are not a true reflection of who we are. The difference between who you are and who you want to be is what you do. It is especially during these times that we need to call upon our faith even more in spite of what we are thinking and feeling.

Faith is the key element that enables us to overcome and makes Fresh Hope different than other recovery models. From our perspective, our faith is what enables us to not lose hope, and in fact is our source of hope even at the most hopeless times of our journey. Faith in Christ not only is the source of our hope; it gives to us the power to renew our minds (Romans 12:2). Because of Christ, our hope and faith, we do not simply live our lives "coping" with a mental illness; instead we live out our lives in wellness despite our mental health issue(s).

We see Fresh Hope as an environment where people listen, where people share only from their perspective. We don't preach at each other. We don't tell each other how to do something, what to believe, or how to respond. We encourage one another, and we share our journey with one another. We do challenge one another at times. But it's a safe environment. It's a safe environment where equipping people to successfully manage (self-empowered wellness) their mood disorder is the goal.

Fresh Hope is a belief that God can use our brokenness for our good, and that when God uses us, He has a purpose and a plan for our lives, mood disorder or not. Feeling like we're broken and shattered in a million pieces, or not, God has a plan.

In fact, Fresh Hope would have the bias that until we're broken and recognize our brokenness and our need for God, He really can't use us all that much.

In Fresh Hope, we infuse hope and faith that God loves us and empowers us to become victors, and to live as victors in Him, in spite of anything in our lives – maybe most of all, our mood disorders.

What are the goals of Fresh Hope?

The first goal is to empower the person who has a mood disorder to successfully manage his/her recovery, choosing wellness to live happy and fulfilling lives.

The second goal of Fresh Hope is to empower loved ones to understand and appropriately relate to their loved one who has the mood disorder, and come alongside their loved one in recovery, so that they too might enjoy life.

Goal number three is that we provide a safe place for sharing both pain and hope without fear of judgment by anyone. In other words, we want to make it a safe place where self-discovery can happen and people can be honest and transparent with one another.

The fourth goal is really the overarching goal, and that is to offer *healing for the past and hope for the future*.

What's the purpose of this book?

The goal of this book is to help you work through the six basic tenets of Fresh Hope; believing that when implemented in your life, these tenets will empower you to live a full and rich life in spite of your mental health diagnosis.

This book is intended to be used by Fresh Hope participants in working through the tenets, as they are the "keys" to living in spite of one's disorder, and finding joy and fulfillment in life. They are the keys to a successful wellness plan. Additionally, this book may also serve as a personal workbook for individuals who may have never attended a Fresh Hope group meeting but are longing to find more joy and fulfillment in life.

Want to attend a Fresh Hope group meeting?

In order to see if there's a group meeting close to you, go to www.FreshHope.us

What if there's no Fresh Hope group that meets where you live?

Consider starting a group! If you are interested in starting a group, please contact us at info@FreshHope.us, or call at 402.763.9255. We have training available for facilitators of Fresh Hope groups and materials designed for facilitating meetings.

How do you find Fresh Hope support online?

We also have ways to connect online through Facebook with others who either are or have been part of a Fresh Hope group, and also for those who are or have worked through this book as individuals. Simply contact our Fresh Hope office for that information.

About the Tenets

When Fresh Hope was developed, we also developed six tenets, each tenet with four parts. The first paragraph in Tenets I, II, III, IV, V, and VI are for the person with the mood disorder. When we read each tenet within our groups, we either have one person with a mood disorder read that individually, or everyone with a mood disorder reads it. It's geared specifically for them.

The second paragraph of the tenet is for the loved one. Loved ones experience the mental health issue in a different way, and they, too, need hope, support, and direction in order to make their own choices and participate in recovery in a productive way.

The third paragraph outlines what we are going to do together, and how we're going to work together to achieve the tenet.

The fourth part is a Scripture passage to support Biblically what is identified in that tenet.

This book is a workbook/book based upon these six tenets, the heart of the Fresh Hope wellness plan.

At first look, the tenets may seem long and cumbersome, but the purpose will gradually unfold. Each of the tenets can really be boiled down to a very simple understanding.

For example:

Tenet I states the sooner you accept your diagnosis and learn about it, the sooner you can get better. The sooner you get treatment for whatever's going on in your life, the sooner you're going to get better. It's just that simple.

Tenet II has to do with relationships, and that our mood disorders and our dysfunctions have affected the people around us and specifically the people we love. We need to recover not just for our own sake, but for the sake of those who love us, and for the sake of those who have been affected by our mood disorder. That means we're going to have to work on and heal broken relationships. Usually, those of us with mood disorders have had them long enough to experience episodes or difficulties that left a trail of broken relationships with frustrated and hurt people. So, it's important for us to mend those relationships.

Tenet III is about not using our mood disorder as an excuse not to live. It's really a choice, and this is where we start talking about, "therefore I choose to believe." *In spite* of my disorder, I'm going to live a rich and full life, and I'm going to choose to push through. I'm going to choose to get up and keep on keeping on. And I recognize in this tenet the fact that I can't do it by myself. I need others, and having support is better than trying to do it on my own.

Tenet IV addresses the whole concept of hopelessness. Hopelessness comes about for a number of reasons, one of them being a lack of confidence and really, the lack of choosing to be hopeful. Many times, we think hope and feeling hopeful is a feeling, per se, or an emotion, when in fact it's really a decision. We can come together and help one another remember that our joy and our hope alone are in the Lord. Therefore, based upon my faith, I am able to say there is hope, even though I may not feel like it. There is hope.

Tenet V explains that we've got to change how we think and act, and that medicine can only do so much. We have to work alongside our medicine and take responsibility for how we think and act, and get rid of our stinkin' thinkin'. We must change how we react in situations and how we interact in relationships.

Tenet VI reminds us that we can easily allow ourselves to be victims because of our disorder. The bottom line of this tenet is that we're going to choose to be victors through Christ.

At each meeting after the tenets are read, we state one simple purpose for the meeting, and that is to encourage one another to choose God's "Fresh Hope" for daily life and for our future.

It's important to respect that who you see at a Fresh Hope meeting is to remain confidential. I want to encourage you to not talk about who you saw or even in a public setting acknowledge that you saw someone at Fresh Hope. This is a group that needs to have a safe place, and that means confidentiality has to be part of it.

Secondly, we don't repeat what's said in a Fresh Hope group meeting. Never say, "Well, so-and-so said such-and-such at the Fresh Hope group meeting". Or, "Did you know that so-and-so's struggling with this or that"? Christians are notorious for covering up gossip by saying, "I encourage you to pray for" or "pray about." Bringing this out in a public setting is gossip. People don't need to know what to pray about. If the Lord wants them to know, then He lays it on their hearts. The reality is it's really easy to use it as an excuse to pass some piece of information along that's to be kept confidential.

Thirdly, we don't judge, nor do we lecture to, someone about their recovery and what they need to do or not do. We do not judge them from a spiritual perspective. Everyone who comes to a Fresh Hope group meeting is not going to share all the same doctrine. They're not coming from Christianity from the same faith perspective. They may not even be coming at it from a Christian perspective at all. But the facilitator is approaching it from a broad-based Christian perspective. The primary focus of a meeting is not for people to be evangelized or participate in the kinds of things that you might do in a Bible study or do as a Christian group meeting at a church. Instead this is where we're respectful of the fact that there are different beliefs. The only thing we don't apologize for is when we pray together we all pray to the Lord Jesus and to the triune God. Those of a different faith persuasion may bow out at that point, not participate in that part of the meeting, or may pray silently based on their own beliefs. If they're non-believers, they may not want to participate. But in most cases, I've seen where people really appreciate and respect this part of Fresh Hope.

Finally, at the end of the tenets, we promise to one another that we're going to be open to listen, we're going to share, and we're going to grow. Those are three very important things. We want to come with our ears open and our mouths ready to provide words of encouragement and support.

Fresh Hope as a peer group support system is phenomenal. It blows my mind – no pun intended – at how powerful the Fresh Hope experience has been for people and how it's helped them. I know self-help groups help people, but I have never seen lives changed like this in all my years of ministry. Again, while this book is geared towards those who participate in a Fresh Hope group, it can easily be read and used by individuals who desire to be overcomers of their mental health issues through Christ.

It's my prayer that your experience with Fresh Hope is very powerful and healing for you. I pray that it gives you healing for your past and hope for your future, and that you know the God of the universe loves you dearly, and that He in fact has great plans for your life. He has the ability to redeem everything you've been through, including the episodes with your mood disorder. In doing so, He holds you and He cares about you, and He wants to infuse you with His hope, which is always fresh and new every day.

Welcome to wholeness; welcome to a rich and fulfilling life in spite of your diagnosis. Welcome to hope. Fresh Hope!

Gripped by Grace,
Brad Hoefs
Founder of Fresh Hope

[21] Yet this I call to mind
and therefore I have hope:

[22] Because of the LORD's great love we are not consumed,
for His compassions never fail.
[23] They are new every morning;
great is Your faithfulness.
[24] I say to myself, "The LORD is my portion;
therefore I will wait for Him."

[25] The LORD is good to those whose hope is in Him,
to the one who seeks Him;
[26] it is good to wait quietly
for the salvation of the LORD.

Lamentations 3:21-26

INTRODUCTION

The Beginning

Section 1

The Recovery Process
Overcoming the Stigma of Mental Illness

Section 2

OK . . . I'm Not OK
Naming the Monster
Framing the Monster
Taming the Monster
Unchain From the Monster
Reclaiming the Monster's Spoils

Section 1

The Recovery Process

Y ou and I likely have something in common: a time when either you or a loved one recognized that something about your behavior just wasn't quite "right." That was the beginning – the *awareness* that you "weren't OK." Next, we began a process of *discovery*. Some people ran straight to a psychiatrist; others visited a therapist, family doctor, or pastor; some read books or did online research. Hopefully, our discoveries led to a place of *acceptance*, and eventually to a place of *healing*. This is the process of Recovery: a continual cycle of Awareness, Discovery, Acceptance, and Healing.

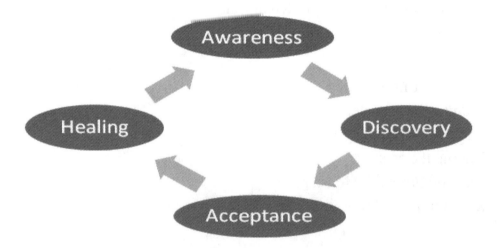

Fig. 1: The Recovery Cycle

The Fresh Hope Tenets begin with *awareness*. We admit that our lives are affected by a mood disorder. This sounds simple, but can be the most difficult part of recovery. No one wants to admit they "aren't ok." No one wants the label of a mental illness. No one wants to feel the stigma of mental illness.

Overcoming the Stigma of Mental Illness

Unfortunately, there is still a certain amount of social stigma regarding mental disorders. We may think back to old movies stereotypes, or remember hearing the hushed tones of people talking about someone with a mental disorder. These memories have contributed to our own individual stigmas. Yes, the first stigma you encounter is most often your own.

Most stigmas are based on mental health care of the past. Today's mental health care has improved greatly. More medications and treatments are available than ever before, and public opinion regarding psychiatric medications are more positive. More than 83% now believe that medications help people deal with day-to-day stresses (Dr. Ramin Mojtabai, *Americans' Attitudes Toward Psychiatric Medications: 1998-2006*, Psychaitric Services, ©August, 2009).

What actually defines mental illness? "The term *mental illness* refers collectively to all diagnosable mental disorders. Effects of the illness include sustained abnormal alterations in thinking, mood, or behavior associated with distress and impaired functioning. The effects of mental illnesses include disruptions of daily function; incapacitating personal, social, and occupational impairment; and premature death. The most common mental illnesses in adults are anxiety and mood disorders" (Centers for Disease Control and Prevention (CDC), Morbidity and Mortality Weekly Report (MMWR) *Mental Illness Surveillance Among Adults in the United States*, September 2, 2011).

Mood disorders are a biological condition involving brain chemistry and genetics. They do not arise from character flaws, lack of faith, or poor choices. Mood disorders are a medical condition. There is no more shame here than if we had diabetes, arthritis, or any other medical ailment. Look at it this way: let's say you've developed breast cancer (don't show your stigmas – men can develop breast cancer also!). Your doctor tells you that there is an excellent survival rate if you have a mastectomy and chemotherapy. Would you say, "I think I'll just try harder to get rid of it on my own?" Of course not! Would you say, "Oh what's the point; I might as well give up and die?" I hope not! Would you live out the rest of your years saying "Oh, there must be something wrong with me because I got breast cancer?" No!

It is logical, reasonable, and sensible to treat medical disorders. This includes mental disorders. The sooner you overcome your inner stigma about mental illness, the faster and healthier your recovery will be. The longer you hold off, the sicker you'll become.

Think about your personal view of mental disorders. Which of the following have contributed to your current views? Use either a "**+**" or a "**-**" in the blank to indicate either a positive or negative influence.

_____ Parents/Family   _____ News/Media

_____ People I've known (with disorder) _____ Movies/Fiction books

_____ Attitudes of friends   _____ Mental Health websites

_____ Mental Health professionals   _____ Medical professionals

_____ Church/Christian teaching   _____ Personal experience

_____ Other _____

Section 2

OK . . . I'm Not OK

Sometimes, we aren't ready to admit we're "not OK" until the disorder causes a major disruption in our lives. A person with bipolar disorder may have some impulsive, risk-taking behavior, and end up encountering the law. A person with depression may spend too many days in bed and end up losing his/her job. A person with social anxiety may be so fearful of large groups he/she misses special family events. Some people will not admit they "aren't OK" until their lives become totally disrupted. I know, because that's what happened to me.

For a number of years I know something was wrong with me. I wasn't sure what it was. I knew that I struggled with an emotional intensity not experienced by the average person. I knew I could get more work done by staying up for five straight days than most people could do in a month. I knew I could feel wired up with boundless energy, yet feel depressed inside. Even so, it took an encounter with the law during a manic episode to convince me I really was "not OK."

Naming the Monster

When I was diagnosed with bipolar disorder, I was relieved, even thrilled that the monster I had lived with and tried to control for so long had a "name." You see, until then I had been worried the doctors and therapists would discover that *I was* the monster. Naming the monster brought so much relief. "It" was the underlying reason for the trail of broken trust, damaged relationships, unexplainable behavior, and humiliating circumstances. I didn't want my life to become unmanageable and hopeless. I didn't want to hurt my family or leave a path of destruction behind me. I didn't choose this disorder – it chose me. No, it wasn't an excuse for what happened. Rather, it was an explanation for my behavior. Finally, there was hope! The good news was that *I wasn't* the monster. After this good news, the task was to discover the nature of the beast. If I was going to have victory over the monster, I needed to understand it.

Framing the Monster

Coming to terms with a mood disorder is one thing; understanding it is a completely different story. I'm a pastor, not a physician. I deal with the spiritual, not the physical. I had no idea the amount of anatomy, biology, and chemistry lessons I would encounter over the next few years. That's a tall order for those of us who did everything possible to avoid science classes in school!

The bottom line that everyone must understand is this: mood disorders involve the improper functioning of the brain. The brain is an organ; just like your heart or kidneys. Mood disorders are a biological, medical problem – a disease of the brain. Mood disorders are *not* due to a lack of self-control or spiritual weakness. But a mood disorder *will* affect one's behavior, and is the explanation for your behavior. However, there will be people who insist you are making excuses for your behavior. Remember, the difference between an "excuse" and an "explanation" is *scientific* proof – and there is plenty of scientific information available. But for our discussion we'll keep it as simple as possible.

Mood disorders, including bipolar disorder and depression, are biological disorders that occur in specific areas of the brain where moods, thinking, sleep, appetite, and behavior are controlled (Bressert, 2011). Scientists have also discovered that the amygdala and the hippocampus (located in the brain) play significant roles in most anxiety disorders, PTSD (Post Traumatic Stress Disorder), ADHD (Attention Deficit Hyperactivity Disorder, and OCD (Obsessive Compulsive Disorder), (National Institute of Mental Health, 2009). Mood disorders involve a dysfunction (like a misfiring, as with a spark plug in a car) of certain neurotransmitters (chemical messengers in our brain). When these neurotransmitters misfire, our moods are changed, our thinking is distorted, we lack control over our impulses, and we are not ourselves (National Institute of Mental Health, 2010).

One last thing I want to mention regarding diagnosis is that sometimes there **is** **no** conclusive diagnosis. You might be told you have some components of anxiety, or mixed moods, or a "type" of mood disorder, but it may not be specific.

This is perfectly reasonable, as your recovery will focus on the *symptoms,* not the *diagnosis.* Your doctor will consider medications that address your symptoms, and your therapy will address the behavioral areas in which you want to improve. Also, the diagnosis you receive may vary from one professional to another. This is also perfectly reasonable. Your diagnosis could vary depending on your current mood and the treatments and therapies you're using, what's going on in your life, or how you describe your symptoms. As we'll discuss later, you don't want to get hung up on the "label" of the diagnosis. The important thing is that you realize something is wrong which keeps you from getting better. You admit you're "not OK" – whatever that means.

Taming the Monster

Medical explanations can sound complicated for laypeople like you and me; but in practice, mood disorders are relatively easy to treat with a combination of medicines, therapies, support, and faith. Yes, this monster *can* be tamed, caged, and even silenced! It is important that you have a trusted medical professional to guide you through the process of education and recovery, as it can be difficult to discern the accuracy of information in the cyber world. Since the treatment of mood disorders involves medications, a psychiatrist (a licensed physician trained in the evaluation and treatment of mental disorders) is the logical choice.

Some people don't like the idea of taking psychotropic medications (chemical substances that affect brain function), while others vow to never live without them. Medications can be the key component in getting better and regaining control of our lives. Medication helps to restore the balance of chemicals in your brain and permit it to function as God intended. Medications are not used to sedate and control us, but rather to restore and enable us. Choose to cooperate with your psychiatrist in finding the right medications and dosages. The longer you fight the diagnosis and medicine, the longer you will remain sick.

Finally, it is important that you find a spiritual support system. I encourage you to find a local church where you can give and receive genuine love and support; a place where you can be open about your disorder without fear of rejection. If you are not already a member of a Fresh Hope support group, consider attending a meeting. If there's not a group near where you live; consider starting a group. Also, anyone working through this workbook is welcome in our private, online community, where you will always find encouragement and support. Unfortunately, not all churches understand mental illness – yet. We are praying and working to that end. We have Fresh Hope support group members who have been terribly hurt by churches who believed that mental illness

Attach yourself firmly to Christ

could only be caused by demonic possession, or that "mental problems" persisted due to the person's lack of faith. If this has happened to you, I want to genuinely tell you I am sorry. Jesus does not shame you. Jesus has never turned His back on you. As you learn to accept your diagnosis, submit to the care of a professional, and surrender to the power and love of Christ, then you *will* begin to see that this monster can be tamed - perhaps even slain!

Unchain From the Monster

In Christ, we find the power to move from being a victim to becoming a victor. For you to experience this victory, there is a critical step you need to take: learn to separate yourself from the disorder. In other words, you need to unchain yourself from the monster and attach yourself firmly to Christ.

You see, left to our own selves, we all fall victim to the god of this world. In this world we will experience sickness, pain, and difficulties because mankind fell into sin in the Garden of Eden. When Adam and Eve disobeyed God and brought original sin into the world, it included sickness, pain, disease, and death. What the church often doesn't understand is that mental illness was included in those maladies. Sin brought sickness and brokenness into the world and separated us from a Holy God, but that's not the end of the story. God made a way for man to "get right" with Him again. Even from the time God banished Adam and Eve from the garden, He promised to provide a way to restore us into a right standing with Him again. No one can live a sinless life. That is, except Jesus, Who came to earth and lived a perfect life and became the perfect sacrifice for the sins of all who would believe in Him. By receiving His sacrifice, we become right with God again and inherit eternal life. In essence, we unchain ourselves from the sinful world we live in and chain ourselves to the cross of Jesus – and when we do that we have His power to overcome the things of this world – including our mental disorder. This doesn't mean all our problems will go away, but we have new power with which to deal with them. Jesus said we would have many problems in this world, but that He came to overcome them (John 17). So, why would you want to remain chained to the monster that sought to destroy you?

Many Christians with mental disorders unknowingly keep themselves chained to the monster and then wonder why God isn't helping them. If we join hands, so to speak, with our disorder and begin to identify with IT rather than with Christ, then IT becomes who you are. It is critical that you learn to separate yourself from the disorder. You are NOT the disorder – you are a new creation in Christ! You are NOT the monster – you have been given the mind of Christ! You are NOT the problem – your DISORDER is the problem. Understanding this concept is essential to a hope-filled journey of recovery!

Words are powerful; spoken words are even more powerful; and words you speak about yourself are the most powerful words ever! Your brain is strongly influenced by the words it hears you speak about yourself. When you say "I am bipolar," or "I struggle with anxiety," or "I battle depression," you give power to the disease. In our Fresh Hope groups we don't say "I'm bipolar"; rather, we say "I've been diagnosed with bipolar disorder." Regardless of your diagnosis, remember this: You are fearfully and wonderfully made, knitted together in your mother's womb by God – and He doesn't make junk! God loves you with an everlasting love. Regardless of your diagnosis, see yourself as God sees you: as a whole person, complete in Christ. Therefore, we no longer identify with the monster; we take on our new identity in Christ.

Reclaiming the Monster's Spoils

If you're still reading, I applaud you for having the courage to come this far! You are obviously serious about regaining control of your life. (You're almost done with the hardest part of recovery!) I hope that above all, you genuinely believe there is *real* hope for your future, but believing that may be harder for some than for others. Some of you may have attempted suicide; perhaps others have broken the law or acted out sexually during a manic episode. Some of you have fallen prey to anxiety or obsessive thinking to the point that you have given up. Some of you may have turned to alcohol or drugs. There may be lost jobs, depleted bank accounts, legal charges, lost opportunities, and lost relationships. Go ahead and take a good, honest look at your life. What you see may look completely different than you envisioned. Consider the damage inflicted from the monster's reign of control. Consider the people relationships that have been affected by your behavior – even though it wasn't your intention to hurt them. Now, be willing to acknowledge and take full responsibility for those actions. You may be wondering why *you* need to take responsibility when you didn't *intend* on hurting anyone – especially if a chemical imbalance in the brain is responsible. Isn't that a good enough excuse? It's an explanation, but not an excuse. The truth is, we remain responsible for real damage – to ourselves and to others. You cannot move forward in your recovery until you take full responsibility for yourself and your past actions. When you deny responsibility for your actions and make excuses for your behavior, you continue to blame others. Then you're stuck in a circle of seeing yourself as a victim and feeling sorry for yourself.

Your life is 10% what happens to you and 90% how you respond. Think back to Nathan's confrontation of King David. 2 Samuel 12:13 tells us that David responded by saying, "I have sinned against the LORD." David responded by taking full responsibility for his actions, and that's what you and I need to do also. Confession is nothing more than agreeing with the Lord. So go to the Lord, mention your specific wrongs, set your mind in agreement with His, and receive His forgiveness.

We are told in Scripture that "If we confess our sins, He is faithful and just, and will forgive us our sins and purify us from all unrighteousness" (1 John 1:9).

Your recovery may also include restoring relationships that have been broken or damaged as a result of your behavior (we'll discuss this in more detail in Chapter 2). For now, rest in the promise of 1 John 1:9 that God will not only forgive your sins, but "purify you from all unrighteousness." This means that you don't have to carry around the guilt and shame of your past actions! And you don't have to live your life thinking "I should have…" "I could have…" Let me warn you, though, that some people find it difficult to let go of the shame and guilt of their past actions. They hold on to the shame as a "motivation" to avoid ever repeating the behavior. Or they carry around the guilt as a form of self-punishment. Don't you dare! When God deems us clean and forgiven – don't argue! We believe Scripture at its face value: "There is now no condemnation for those who are in Christ Jesus" (Romans 8:1). For that reason, Fresh Hope is declared a guilt-free, shame-free zone.

As you accept forgiveness and responsibility, you will be able to live in the shame-free, guilt-free zone of God's grace. I must warn you, however, that not everyone will like that you've moved into that neighborhood – especially those who feel "wronged" by your actions. For me, this was a painful realization. I innocently believed that those whose lives had also been affected by my disorder would understand, and not only be forgiving, but be willing to accept me back with open arms and go on with life "as we knew it." That's not what happened.

Those I had worked with were confused, humiliated, angry, and hurt by my public manic episode prior to my diagnosis. They said that they forgave me, but they made it clear that they did NOT want me to return to work, even if it was just to bring about closure and healing. I was offered the stiff arms of loving Christian rejection. Their message was, "We forgive you. We love you. But, we want nothing more to do with you; even if there's a name for "your monster."

My wife and children were also hurt, humiliated, sad, confused, and grieving – not only by my actions, but by the rejection of those who had been our friends and ministry partners for years. My family was hurt from every direction. Yet, my wife made it very clear to me that she wasn't going anywhere as long as I was committed to getting better. Out of her commitment to the Lord, her love for me, and her understanding of the "monster," she was willing to "hang in there" and move forward in forgiveness, healing, and hope. Along with her, my children, extended family, and a few very close friends, I began the long journey ahead of me.

That was 17 years ago. I am still on that journey today, and will continue to be until the Lord either returns to earth or brings me home. I have experienced rejection, judgment, and humiliation – mostly from people who are supposed to know better. Truly, I can echo the words of Joseph in Genesis 50:20:

> *"As for you, you meant evil against me, but God meant it for good in order to bring about this present result, to preserve many people alive."*

This monster sought to destroy me, but God took that pain and is using it for His good. The monster intended to bring me down, but God has restored me. The monster intended to take my family, but God healed my marriage and my family relationships. This monster intended to silence me, but God has given me a new message – this message of Fresh Hope.

Our God longs to do the same thing for you. "With Him, all things are possible" (Matthew 19:26). Are you ready to reclaim everything that the monster has taken from you? So my friend, pack up all your stigmas, self-pity, and excuses, and say goodbye to your stinkin' thinkin' once and for all!

During my darkest time, I received a card with this poem. It was perfect and it kept me going! I would read it and weep…but, it was so encouraging. It made me be patient with the healing process and what the Lord was doing through my pain.

God Is a Restorer

God's purpose is not to destroy us but to restore us.
The enemy is the destroyer,
but God has promised to restore the things
the enemy has stolen from our lives:
all the years of lost joy,
all the times of frustration and defeat,
all the moments of regret,
all the pains of lost opportunities,
all the hurts of broken relationships.
God is building His kingdom with you –
a kingdom of joy, love, peace,
righteousness, victory, redemption,
and right relationships.

Roy Lessin

This Scripture was on the inside of the card:

"I will repay you for the years the locusts have eaten –
the great locust and the young locust,
the other locusts and the locust swarm –
my great army that I sent among you.
You will have plenty to eat, until you are full,
and you will praise the name of the Lord your God,
Who has worked wonders for you. . ." Joel 2:25-26

Key Thoughts

- Our personal stigmas make it hard to admit we are "not OK."
- Mood disorders are medical conditions.
- Mood disorders do not stem from a character flaw or spiritual weakness, but are a result of brain chemistry and genetics. Mood disorders are a medical condition.
- The sooner you accept that your life has been affected by a mood disorder, the faster and healthier your recovery will be.
- Malfunctioning brain chemistry can affect our reasoning skills and cause us to have distorted thinking about ourselves.
- **Name** the monster. You're NOT the monster. You have a disease.
- **Frame** the monster. See a professional. Learn about your disease.
- **Tame** the monster. Accept the same treatment as you would for any other type of medical disorder.
- **Unchain** from the monster. Separate yourself from your disorder. In Christ, you are made brand new. Walk in that reality.
- **Reclaim** what the monster has taken. Trust God. Trust the others He has put in your life.

CHAPTER ONE

Coming to Terms

TENET I

My life is affected by a mood disorder and can become unmanageable and hopeless, especially if ignored or untreated. Therefore, I choose the help and support of others to overcome the struggles and find more joy in life.

Together, we have understanding. We remind each other of the Lord's love, and that He alone can do all things. He is the source of our hope, and in Him we can overcome all things.

"I can do everything through Him who gives me strength." *Philippians 4:13 (NIV)*

Section 1
Accepting a Mood Disorder Diagnosis
"Nothing is Wrong with Me"
A Biblical Example of Denial

Section 2
"I'm Doomed"

Section 3
"It's Not That Bad"
"No One Understands Me"

Section 4
Making Tenet I Personal

Wrap Up
Q & A With the Psychiatrist

Section 1

Accepting a Mood Disorder Diagnosis

O vercoming your stigma about mental disorders in *general* is one thing, but coming to terms with your *own* mental health diagnosis is a bit more challenging! At one time or another, it is common to have one of the following attitudes:

1. Nothing is wrong with me.
2. I'm doomed.
3. It's not that bad.
4. No one understands me.
5. I might as well just give up (on myself).

These are just a few of the many reactions people have. There is not a right or wrong way to respond. The important thing is that you are honest with yourself and with the people who love you, and that you eventually come to a place of truth and acceptance.

"Nothing is Wrong with Me"

What is denial? No, it's not "a river in Egypt" as the old joke goes. I used to think denial meant you didn't want to *admit* something was true. In fact, denial means you don't even have a clue anything is wrong!

> **Denial** (noun) de·ni·al : a state of mind marked by an inability to recognize and deal with a serious personal problem. (Psychological definition, Encarta Dictionary)

Has there been a time when people thought you weren't acting or thinking correctly, but you didn't agree? It's understandable that people with mood disorders may have this reaction. If we are in a state of bipolar mania, we may have grandiose thinking that keeps us from believing we have any faults. If we're depressed, we may be so inwardly focused that we don't understand how our behavior affects others.

Denial can be common in the early process of discovery. Your loved ones may be telling you that you need help, or that you should "see someone." You may not want to believe anything is wrong, but it is important to consider the words of people who love you. Consider the wise words of King Solomon:

> *"Wounds from a friend can be trusted, but an enemy multiplies kisses."*
> *Proverbs 27:6*

Take a moment to consider what this Scripture verse means to you. How would you apply it to people who love and are concerned for you? Write your thoughts below:

_____

_____

_____

When we are hurt by the words of a loved one, they are often true. Loved ones will risk being honest with us when no one else will. Some people may tell us only what they want us to know, or only what we want to hear. Learn to trust the wounds from a friend.

A Biblical Example of Denial

It's always comforting to discover that the great people of the Bible have the same shortcomings we do. Even King David experienced denial about his behavior, and he was described as "a man after God's own heart" (1 Samuel 13:14). Let's look at David's experience in Chapters 11 and 12 of 2 Samuel.

To sum up the story, King David had extra-marital relations with Bathsheba (the wife of Uriah) and she became pregnant. King David ordered that Uriah (who was a member of King David's army) be positioned "*in the front line of battle where the fighting is fiercest. Then withdraw from him so he will be struck down and die*" (2 Samuel 11:15).

As expected, Uriah was killed in battle. After the proper time of mourning, David and Bathsheba were married. Now, I think most of us would agree that David was obviously in the wrong. Not only had he been with another man's wife, but he had "arranged" for her husband to be killed so he could have Bathsheba for himself.

Nathan, the prophet, knew King David well, and did not approve of his behavior. In 2 Samuel Chapter 12, Nathan confronted David by giving him an "account" of two men; one was a rich man who owned many sheep and cattle, the other was a poor man who had only one little ewe that he deeply loved. Nathan explained that the rich man slaughtered the beloved ewe of the poor man to prepare a meal for a visitor, rather than taking one of his own sheep, of which there were many. Here is the description of King David's response in verses 5-7 of 2 Samuel 12:

> *"David burned with anger against the man and said to Nathan, "As surely as the LORD lives, the man who did this deserves to die! He must pay for that lamb four times over, because he did such a thing and had no pity."*
> *Then Nathan said to David, **"You are the man!"***

We might wonder how David could be described as a "man after God's own heart," yet be so ignorant of his own actions. When King David was confronted with a description of his own actions under the pretense of Nathan's "story," he was outraged! He didn't consider his own behavior until Nathan, a trusted friend, said "You are the man!" King David knew that "the wounds of a friend can be trusted."

What qualities must have been present in the relationship for King David to accept Nathan's accusation?

_____

_____

_____

Do you have relationships with these qualities? If so, with whom?

_____

_____

_____

King David's response demonstrated his true character. He acknowledged his actions, confessed, and accepted the consequences. Again, remember that our lives are 10% what happens to us, and 90% how we respond. David demonstrated how easy it is to live in denial about our own behavior. More importantly, he demonstrated that, when confronted, our response is far more important. Better stated by Robert Tew, "Strength of character isn't always about how much you can handle before you break. It's also about how much you can handle after you've broken."

Do you have a "Nathan" in your life? What are they telling you about your behavior? Do you agree?

_____

_____

_____

How have you responded? Do you trust their motive?

_____

_____

_____

Perhaps your concerns about something "not being right" are coming from within yourself rather than from someone else.

Are you willing to do what it takes to look for an answer? If not, what is stopping you?

_____

_____

_____

Other people may not have all the answers. You may not have all the answers. Your heavenly Father, Who loves you and knows everything about you, has the answers. Are you willing to hear from Him? Take time to read Psalm 139 in your Bible. Then pray, using your own words, or the example below:

Heavenly Father, You created me and know my innermost being. You love me and have a plan for my life. Holy Spirit, search me and know my ways. Allow me the courage to be honest with myself and see myself through Your eyes. Lord, give me the humility to consider the words of those who love me. Above all, give me the grace to admit my shortcomings and strength to change them with Your Help. Amen.

What have you learned about yourself in this section? Record your thoughts below:

_____

_____

_____

Section 2

"I'm Doomed"

Those who respond to a mood disorder with an "I'm doomed!" attitude believe that their diagnosis confirms what they've always feared - that one day they'll be living in their car eating government surplus food, or they'll spend 14 hours a day finger-painting butterflies in an institution. After all, people who are "normal" don't have a psychiatric diagnosis. Right?

The fact is, over 75 million Americans are affected by mental illness. That means "nearly *one in three* Americans are diagnosed with a mental disorder in any given year. Substance disorders - like alcoholism - are recognized in the rest of the world as a mental disorder, and are included as such. If you don't think mental illness will impact your life, you're sadly mistaken. If it doesn't hit you, it's going to hit some-one you love or are close to." (John M Grohol, PSYD, "Mental Health Statistics", *World of Psychology*, http://psychcentral.com, May 3, 2010)

According to the World Health Organization, mental illness results in more disabil-ity in developed countries than any other group of illnesses, including cancer and heart disease. The most common mental illnesses in adults are anxiety and mood disorders. Nearly 50% of U.S. adults will develop at least one mental illness during their lifetime. (Centers for Disease Control and Prevention (CDC), Morbidity and Mortality Weekly Report (MMWR) *Mental Illness Surveillance Among Adults in the United States*, Supplements, September 2, 2011 / 60(03);1-32).

Did you know that mood disorders are one of the most easily treated medical condi-tions? It doesn't happen overnight and it takes effort on your part, but you *can* live with minimal, if any, effects of the mood disorder in your life. The combination of medications, talk therapy, support, and faith make it possible to manage your moods proactively – and that means your moods don't control you; **you** control your moods.

In fact, your life will be better than ever as you come to terms with your diagnosis and learn to live your life *in spite* of your disorder. That is the sole focus of Fresh Hope.

I founded Fresh Hope as a person with a mood disorder, who just happened to be a pastor. My faith has taught me to look at my circumstances from God's perspective, which includes my view on mental illness. Most recovery groups slip a few Biblical principles into a medical model for recovery, but Fresh Hope *begins* with the Biblical principles and incorporates the medical and therapeutic components. Dr. Caroline Leaf, a Cognitive Neuroscientist, states, "Science is catching up with the Bible." Don't get me wrong, we place high value on psychiatry, medicines, and therapy. In fact we have professionals who review our materials and serve on our Board. However, when faith is at the forefront of your recovery program, you can do more than *manage* your disorder; you can *overcome* and live a hope-filled, joyous, purposeful life. With Jesus Christ, you are *never* doomed!

Why might someone feel their life is "doomed" when they are told they have a mood disorder? Do you feel doomed?

In Fresh Hope, we learn to recognize both our moods and our "hope tank." Our hope tank is simply the amount of hope (or lack of hopelessness) we are able to choose at any given time. See, hope is a decision based upon Who the Lord is, and not based upon how you feel. You have to choose the sure and certain hope found only in Jesus. We'll go into this in greater detail in Chapter 4. You might hear someone say, "My mood is a 3, but my hope tank is full." This person has learned that regardless of the situation, they know the mood and/or symptoms will pass.

When you first suspected you "weren't OK," how full was your hope tank?

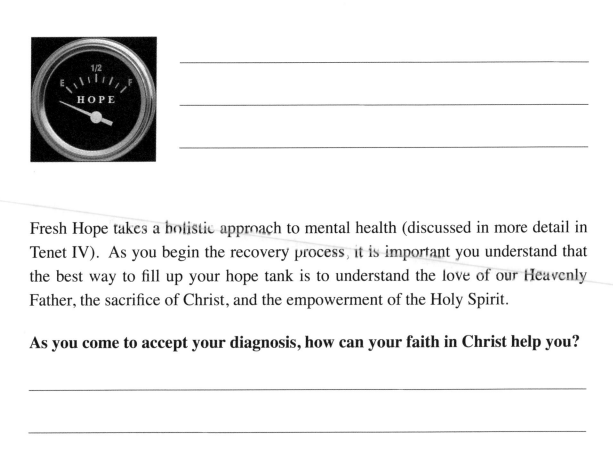

Fresh Hope takes a holistic approach to mental health (discussed in more detail in Tenet IV). As you begin the recovery process, it is important you understand that the best way to fill up your hope tank is to understand the love of our Heavenly Father, the sacrifice of Christ, and the empowerment of the Holy Spirit.

As you come to accept your diagnosis, how can your faith in Christ help you?

Section 3

"It's Not That Bad"

It's easy for those of us with mood disorders to think others are making too much fuss about our behavior. Some people will acknowledge feeling a little "off" but draw the line at giving "it" a name. For example, a close friend who has stood by me through my own mental health struggles informed me that he didn't have a mood disorder like me. Yet he was severely clinically depressed and he was taking medicine. He told me that he "wasn't sick like me," he said, "but just depressed!" (He saw me as having mental illness, but did not see "just" depression as a mental illness.) Yet this depression has taken quite a toll on his life, causing job losses and a destroyed marriage. Still, the stigma of being labeled as someone with a mood disorder or mental illness was unthinkable for him. Often, recovery is less work than the hopeless campaign of trying to convince everyone you're "OK." Why not just admit you're "not OK," and let the healing begin? It's not who you are that holds you back – it's who you think you're not.

"No One Understands Me"

Those of us with a mood disorder may think others don't understand us because we think either too highly or too lowly of ourselves. Perhaps you've heard yourself say something like, "You could never handle my life" or "You'd be doing a lot worse if you were in my place." People with mental disorders are often highly intelligent and creative people. We may think that we are either more important or have experienced deeper pain than others because of our circumstances.

On the flip side, we also demonstrate the "no one understands me" attitude by believing we're the only "normal" one. Before I came to accept my own bipolar diagnosis, I had convinced everyone around me that *they* needed therapy. I believed that I wasn't the one with the problem, they were!

It's true that no one understands the exact circumstances and feelings that we experience – but that doesn't mean we're OK. When a mood disorder is at work, our brain chemistry is out of whack and our reasoning can malfunction. Our mind can play tricks on us. What others so plainly see can seem absurd to us. Our greatest threat may lie in believing everything our brain tells us. Acceptance begins when we understand that *our distorted thinking* contributes to the way we see ourselves and respond to others.

Don't believe everything your brain tells you

Tenet I

Each Fresh Hope meeting begins with the reading of our six Tenets. Tenet I is the focus of this chapter, and I hope that the reading thus far has brought you to a point where you can fully accept everything this encompasses.

Let's look at the first sentence of Tenet I:

> ***My life is affected by a mood disorder and can become unmanageable and hopeless, especially if ignored or untreated.*** Therefore, I choose the help and support of others to overcome the struggles and find more joy in life.

Do you agree with this statement? Let's look at each thought separately:

My life is affected by a mood disorder

Have you worked through any roadblocks that have prevented you from accepting your diagnosis? Can you acknowledge that you have a mood disorder without feeling shame or stigma?

_____

_____

and can become unmanageable and hopeless

Are you willing to acknowledge that your mood disorder has affected the quality of your life, making it hard to manage and leading to (or potentially leading to) hopelessness and broken relationships? If so, how?

_____

_____

especially if ignored or untreated.

Do you understand both the ease and importance of treating a mental disorder just as if you had another medical condition?

_____

_____

I hope you were able to fully accept those statements. If not, give yourself some time. If you can only commit to one thing, commit to learning. Share openly with others who have mood disorders and are living in sustained recovery. Ask about their recovery. Ask how their life is different. Ask what has helped them.

In most cases, when someone is suffering from a mood disorder or mental illness, denial will cause strained relationships with others. Damage may have been done and will not be corrected until there is acceptance of the diagnosis.

When you consider the damage that has occurred because of your mood disorder, what specific things come to mind? Record them here:

Ways I have hurt myself:

_____

_____

_____

_____

_____

How I have hurt others:

_____

_____

_____

_____

_____

Now, bring your list before the Lord in prayer. If there are sins, acknowledge them and ask for the Lord's forgiveness. If your list includes bad choices and bad decisions, acknowledge them and ask the Lord to help you find a way to make those things right. Finally, ask the Lord to help you forgive yourself and live in the truth of His love and forgiveness.

You can write your own prayer below, or pray something like this:

Dear Heavenly Father, as I look at my actions I confess that I have sinned against you by (specifically name sins). I accept Christ's sacrifice for my sin and ask for Your forgiveness. Thank You for Your promise to both forgive and cleanse me from my sin. Help me see my actions through Your eyes. Transform my mind and renew my thinking so that I may walk blameless in your sight. In Jesus name I pray. Amen.

Write out a prayer in your own words:

_____

_____

_____

_____

_____

Now let's look at the second sentence of Tenet I:

> My life is affected by a mood disorder and can become unmanage-able and hopeless, especially if ignored or untreated. ***Therefore, I choose the help and support of others to overcome the struggles and find more joy in life.***

If you have been honest with yourself this far, you will have acknowledged that your actions have hurt others. You will also have realized that treating your disorder will most likely involve other people, including a psychiatrist, therapist, and support group. Sometimes it's hard to admit we need help, and even more difficult to ask for it.

Look at it this way; it's impossible to know everything. Even the most brilliant doctor in the world has an accountant. Even the most accurate accountant has a plumber. Even the best plumber has a dentist. And so on, and so on... The point is, you may know everything about something, but you can't know something about everything. Trust others. You've got to trust an expert on the brain, an expert on behavior, and people who are experts on YOU! Accepting the help of others is going to make YOU a healthier person.

Asking for help is not a sign of weakness; it's a sign of strength. Consider the Apostle Paul, who writes in the 2nd book of Corinthians, Chapter 12:

> [7]*"To keep me from becoming conceited because of these surpassingly great revelations, there was given me a thorn in my flesh, a messenger of Satan, to torment me.* [8] *Three times I pleaded with the Lord to take it away from me.* [9] *But he said to me, "My grace is sufficient for you, for my power is made perfect in weakness". Therefore I will boast all the more gladly about my weaknesses, so that Christ's power may rest on me.* [10] *That is why, for Christ's sake, I delight in weaknesses, in insults, in hardships, in persecutions, in difficulties. For when I am weak, then I am strong.*

Asking for help is not a sign of weakness

There was something Paul described as "a thorn in my flesh," something wrong with his body that tormented him. Scholars have speculated as to what the ailment was, but God may have kept that a mystery so that you and I could identify with Paul. In a sense, we could say that our mood disorder is the "thorn in our flesh."

When Paul asked the Lord to remove the thorn, what was the Lord's response (verse 9)?

It's as if we can choose to deal with the "thorns" in our own strength, or with the Lord's strength. You've often heard people say "the Lord will never give you more than you can handle." I don't agree. Often He will give you just enough so that you realize your need for Him. But He will never give you more than the two of you *together* can handle. He wants you to depend on Him. Noted speaker Joyce Meyer states it well: "God doesn't just want to give you strength. He wants to *be* your

31

strength!" He doesn't want you to show Him how strong you can be – He wants to show you how strong He can be through you. Are you willing to accept His strength?

In verse 9, why does Paul say he will delight in his own weakness?

_____

_____

We acknowledge our weakness by admitting our human limitations. In admitting our limitations, we acknowledge that only God knows everything about everything. When we trust him, His strength takes over, and His power becomes evident in our weakness.

Now look again at the second part of Tenet I:

> My life is affected by a mood disorder and can become unmanageable and hopeless, especially if ignored or untreated. *Therefore, I choose the help and support of others to overcome the struggles and find more joy in life.*

Can you admit your own limitations and allow God to give you the strength you need?

_____

_____

Can you agree that you need the help of professionals?

_____

_____

Can you accept the support of people the Lord has (and will) put in your life to learn to live (and thrive) with your mood disorder?

_____

_____

Key Thoughts

- Denial is not pretending you don't *know* something's wrong, it's not having a clue there *is* anything wrong.
- Loved ones will risk being honest with you when no one else will – so, listening to them is important as they are most likely providing accurate feedback to you.
- It's not what happens to us, but how we *respond* that determines our true character.
- One out of three adults is affected by a mood disorder.
- Mood disorders are one of the most easily treated medical conditions.
- You can learn to live a fulfilling life despite your mood disorder.
- Christ makes the difference between "managing" your disorder and "overcoming" your disorder.

Section 4

Making Tenet I Personal

Consider what the words of Tenet I mean to you personally. In the exercise below, rewrite Tenet I to reflect your own life situation. Be as specific as you can.

For example:

Fresh Hope Tenet I

My life is affected by a mood disorder and can become unmanageable and hopeless, especially if ignored or untreated. Therefore, I choose the help and support of others to overcome the struggles and find more joy in life.

John's Tenet I

My life has been controlled by depression to the point that I cannot control my own thoughts and actions if left untreated. Therefore, I choose the help and support of Dr. Shaw, medicine, Fresh Hope, and my family to overcome my struggles and find more joy in life.

My Tenet I

_____

_____

_____

_____

Every time you read Tenet I, remember these words you have written, and take pride in the courage and honesty you admitted to start this journey of recovery. Well done.

Q & A with the Psychiatrist

Dr. Michael Egger is a psychiatrist and serves on the Board of Fresh Hope. He has been my doctor and encourager for almost 20 years. I have asked him to provide his professional input on questions often associated with mental health issues. Each chapter will end with a question & answer section with Dr. Egger to help you better understand the key points.

1. If mood disorders are due to brain chemistry and genetics, why doesn't everyone in my family have the same problems I have?

    Dr. Egger: Not all forms of mood disorders are directly inherited, but bipolar affective disorder is transmitted as autosomal dominant with incomplete penetrance which means that children of a patient with bipolar affective disorder will have the gene, but not necessarily the full mood disorder, some showing virtually no symptoms at all and others only a very mild form of it.

2. Why did no one discover I had this disorder earlier in my life?

    Dr. Egger: Mood disorders are not fully symptomatic until late adolescence or early adult life. The earlier the symptoms show up in life most likely the more severe will be the full symptom pattern as it develops. Bipolar disorder appearing in childhood with severe irritability, mood swings, and pressured thinking is sometimes reported before age 12, generally suggesting a severe form of the disorder.

3.   Who can make a mental health diagnosis? How is it done? Are there tests?

Dr. Egger: Physicians including psychiatrists and licensed clinical psychologists may make a mental health diagnosis. In some states, other levels of therapist may also. The diagnosis is made with a clinical interview, sometimes supplemented with paper/pencil tests to reveal certain symptom groups such as depression and mania rating scales, the MMPI (Minnesota Multiphasic Personality Inventory) and Connor's Inventory for ADHD.

CHAPTER TWO

The Ripple Effect

TENET II

My mood disorder has also affected my relationships and the lives of those around me. Therefore, I choose to overcome for both my own good, and the good of those who love me.

Together, we commit to speaking the truth in love, healing broken relationships and viewing each other as the Lord views us.

"So let's pursue those things which bring peace and which are good for each other." Romans 14:19 (God's Word Translation, 1995)

Section 1
Messy Relationships
God's Desire for our Relationships

Section 2
How Mood Disorders Affect Relationships

Section 3
Why We Make Amends

Section 4
How We Make Amends

Section 5
Making Tenet II Personal

Wrap Up
Q & A with the Psychiatrist

Section 1

Messy Relationships

T he second Fresh Hope Tenet begins by acknowledging that people with mood disorders often create messy relationships. Many important relationships are already damaged before a mood disorder is first diagnosed. There may be a long trail of failed relationships over many years, an abrupt shattering of longstanding relationships, or both. This leads to pain for people with mood disorders and for their loved ones. If you have a mood disorder, you've likely experienced something between strained relationships and a shattering of your relationships. There is good news, though. Healing and recovery are possible. With treatment and hard work you can overcome the symptoms of your mood disorder, and relationships can be healed.

One reason that damaged relationships cause pain in our lives is because God designed people to be connected with one another in harmony. He desires that we live together in unity and peace. Later in this chapter, we'll get into how to repair damaged relationships. But before we do, let's look at what God says about how He intended our relationships to look.

God's Desire for Relationships

Look up and complete these Bible Verses.

- John 13:34 A new command I give to you, that you _____ one another.

- Romans 14:19 Let us therefore make every effort to do what leads to _____ and to mutual edification.

- Romans 15:7 _____ one another, then, just as Christ accepted you, in order to bring praise to God.

- Galatians 5:13 You, my brothers, were called to be free. But do not use your freedom to indulge the sinful nature; rather, serve one another in _____.

- Galatians 6:2 _____ each other's burdens, and in this way you will fulfill the law of Christ.

- Ephesians 4:25 Therefore each of you must put off falsehood and speak _____ to his neighbor, for we are all members of one body.

- Ephesians 4:32 Be kind and compassionate to one another, _____ each other, just as in Christ God forgave you.

- 1 Thessalonians 5:11 Therefore _____ one another and _____ _____ _____, just as in fact you are doing.

- James 5:16 Therefore, _____ your sins to each other and _____ for each other so that you may be healed. The prayer of a righteous man is powerful and effective.

- 1 Peter 4:9 Offer _____ to one another without grumbling.

The above verses are just a sampling of over 50 commands calling us to love one another and live together in harmony.

If you're feeling convicted by these passages, you don't need to feel embarrassed or ashamed. We are all a work in progress. As we're growing, it's helpful to remember that God never changes. In His infinite love and wisdom, God gave us these Words to help us grow and experience true community and fellowship. There is encouragement in knowing that we can change; that God offers forgiveness when we ask. He offers us new beginnings. That means your relationships with others can change to be molded in the pattern of these verses!

Why do you think the Bible places so much emphasis on these "one another" commands?

_____

_____

_____

_____

Describe how you can apply what you have read to your relationships with others:

_____

_____

_____

_____

Section 2

How Mood Disorders Affect Relationships

It's important to consider how the mood disorder has contributed to strains in your relationships with others. To a large degree, it's much like any other serious illness within a family or within a group of friends. There's a ripple effect when a person suffers from any kind of ongoing serious illness – and the same is true with mood disorders. Why? Well, let's just say someone has a serious chronic disorder such as muscular dystrophy, or is in a serious car accident and becomes a paraplegic. It's going to change the whole family dynamic. It's going to change nearly everything. The same is true with a mood disorder. It affects our behavior. It changes how we interact. It changes the way we do things. This is especially true when not managed, when we're not medicated, and when the mood disorder is not being treated. It certainly changes the lives of those around us.

As painful as it is to think about, consider how various aspects of your mood disorder have affected your loved ones – either prior to being diagnosed or every time you have an episode or difficulty or setback. For instance, if you've attempted suicide, think about how that makes the people around you feel. My wife and I know exactly how that feels, in fact more so than just a suicide *attempt*. Rather, we experienced the suicide of my mother-in-law. And I watched my wife go through the pain and agony of losing her mother to suicide. We had a therapist at the time tell us when someone loses a loved one to suicide there's really two different processes of grieving going on. One has to do with the loss of the person themselves – the death itself; and the other has to do to with the grieving that's going on because of not understanding why he/she would take their own life. That affects everyone. Will you commit that – no matter what – you won't attempt to take your life? Remember, our actions have consequences that reach far beyond ourselves.

There are lots of other troubles commonly experienced by people with mood disorders and their loved ones. There may be financial burdens, unemployment, hospital stays, or even legal troubles. While these things can seem overwhelming, they can all be overcome. It's hard work. But it's worth it. And you can do it.

When I was at my worst, there were so many times I wanted to simply give up and give in. I'd gone through a horrific public episode of manic behavior. I was humiliated and overwhelmed. Although I didn't see it this way at the time, it was like this single event sent a shock wave throughout all of my relationships and all of my thinking. My thoughts were scrambled, and I was so fatigued. I wanted healing, but I was scared – scared that I would never fully recover; that I would never be the same in my own eyes or the eyes of others.

I knew there were things I needed to change. But I didn't know where to begin. I had hurt so many people and I was sickened and saddened by the whole ordeal – especially my behavior during the manic episode, the myriad ways that it had hurt others, and the misunderstandings that might never completely go away.

To make matters worse, many people had turned their backs on me. They would say they loved me but they basically wanted nothing more to do with me. Or they said they had forgiven me but I was broken merchandise that they could no longer trust the way they had before. I found I shared an element of life with author J.K. Rowling, who said, "Rock bottom became the solid foundation on which I rebuilt my life".

Fortunately, there were many people who had not given up on me. Among them were close friends and my immediate family, including my wife and my children. That was a true blessing for me.

What about you? Think about your closest relationships – the friends and family members who are closest to you now. **Consider how your mood disorder has affected these relationships. In the first blank, list a person with whom you have a significant relationship (such as your spouse, parents, children, friends, co-workers). Then describe the ways the mood disorder has affected the relationship.** Remember, the point is not to make excuses for your behavior or to cast blame on anyone. Instead, try taking an objective look at some of your important relationships in light of what you have learned about yourself and the condition with which you have been diagnosed.

Effects on my relationship with _____:

Effects on my relationship with _____:

Effects on my relationship with _____:

Effects on my relationship with _____:

Effects on my relationship with _____:

Describe some things you have learned about yourself and your relationships with others:

_____

_____

_____

_____

_____

Section 3

Why We Make Amends

Probably the most painful thing to come to terms with, for me, was the fact that my mood disorder had affected, literally, thousands of people. Most of all, it had affected those closest to me that I loved so dearly and who were so mistreated and bumped and bruised by me and by others because of my mood disorder and my manic episodes. See, the truth is: not only have our lives been affected by our mood disorders, but so also the lives of our loved ones.

We all understand that if there's alcoholism in a family everyone in that family is affected by the alcoholism. There are people who might say, "Well, it's the alcoholic," but the reality is it's the *alcoholism*. And if somebody has a mental illness or a mood disorder, it's the *mood disorder* that's the issue – not the person. Separating the mood disorder from the person can be hard to do because the disorder affects the person's behavior. But it can be done.

Like other serious medical conditions, a mental issue can drain the family very quickly. It becomes the center of attention. This can be very painful to come to terms with, but it can also be very encouraging when you understand that it need not stay this way when one is successfully empowered for living a life of wellness.

There were times where the only thing that motivated me to get better – the only reason I could pull myself out of bed or force myself to even do something as mundane as getting up and staying up for several hours – was my wife and children. There were many times I did what I needed to do to recover for the sake of those who loved me, because my bipolar disorder had affected *them*. And while I could not bring myself to do what I needed to do for *me*, I was motivated to at least do it for *them*.

Although it's taken a lot of work, I'm pleased to say that my relationships have never been healthier. I've never been happier. A lot of people would look at my life, if they don't know me, and from a distance say, "Oh my gosh, that guy failed – he fell apart, crashed and burned, and his life has never been the same." It's true that things may look different – they may even look, from an earthly perspective, like I failed. But the truth is this: after I crashed and burned, by God's grace I got back up. He gave me a fresh start. I found my hope to get up and start again in Him! And that made all the difference. Now, things have never been better for me.

It was hard work to get back up. It was hard to work through the pain. It was hard to work on the relationships of those who didn't give up on me. It took a lot of time to work through the pain and relationship issues with them. It was worth it, though. As I look back, I now see that hard work as an investment. It is paying dividends that I could have never imagined: lasting friendships and rich relationships that are worth more than their weight in gold (and it's tax free, too!).

I'm thrilled to say that there are now two people in my life that have never been negatively affected by my mood disorder. In fact, they have benefited from me having gone through all the stuff and experienced a lot of emotional healing, mental growth, and successful management of my mood disorder. Those two people are my grandchildren. And when I'm around them, I'm reminded of how much it was worth it to go through the pain of recovery. It's worth it, my friend. It's worth it!

You might feel alone. You might have a long line of broken relationships lying in ruins behind you. Or, maybe you haven't enjoyed close relationships with others before. If that's the case, you can be encouraged that there are others like you who also yearn for friendship. As you seek recovery for your mood disorder you will find that it's easier to connect with others and enter into the type of meaningful relationships that we've been describing. That can be very motivating.

Read and paraphrase the following Scripture passages.

Matthew 5:21-25

_____

_____

_____

_____

Matthew 18:21-35

_____

_____

_____

In your own words, describe how these passages address broken or strained relationships:

_____

_____

_____

Section 4

How We Make Amends

What does it mean to make amends? It means for you and me to take responsibility– going to the people that we have hurt and asking for forgiveness and doing what we can to restore the relationship. Scripture tells us that we're to try and make peace with everyone as best we can, to do everything we can on our part (Romans 12:18). There are times when the other person won't do that, but we have to do what we can, and then we have to let it go.

Sometimes we need to make amends with people who aren't safe, and therefore we need to process that with a mediator (such as a pastor, counselor, or peer support specialist) and figure out how to best go about that – whether that's with a third person or through a letter. And sometimes it's making amends with someone who's no longer alive; and again, that can be done with a mediator. But in making amends, God has the opportunity to restore the relationship. Making amends is about reconciliation, restoration, and healing. God is all about picking up the pieces and making something new. And no, that relationship will never be the same, but now it has the opportunity to be better than it was. Making amends is a positive thing. It's part of how God, piece by piece, person by person, redeems our past.

Everybody hurts each other. Everybody does it. Everyone has relationship issues, but not everybody makes amends. Mood disorders usually exacerbate relationship issues. So because of our illnesses, or because of our mood disorders, we tend to have a lot of relationships that are broken – a lot of people who have been hurt. So we have an opportunity to do a lot of mending. It's a good thing. And that fear that you might have, or that anxiety you might have about it, well, you just have to push through it sometimes.

You start with the person who is the closest and safest for you. Each time you make amends you get stronger, and you begin to see more and more each time how God is redeeming your past and healing you. It can be so positive, because once you begin to manage those relationships those people are there for you in ways you can't even imagine. And those relationships become such a rich blessing and source of joy and encouragement. I can't even tell you how much joy I have in my relationships these days. They're everything for me. Relationships used to be the source of contention in my life. I would run away from people. I would isolate because I got so agitated and irritated all the time. And today I run towards people because I enjoy the relationships and the connection.

It's likely that, to cope with your moods, you've developed some addictions or behaviors that are very unhealthy. That too affects everyone around you. Sometimes it's a dual diagnosis because there is alcoholism or drug addiction. It might be unusual or bizarre behaviors or just dysfunctional behaviors that we thought were helpful when we were undiagnosed or in crisis. And all of those things have to be worked through because they caused pain. Everyone around us who loves and cares about us also feels that hurt and pain. If other conditions are present such as alcoholism or similar addictions, you'll need the help of a counselor or therapist to work through them in addition to your mood disorder.

The good news in all of this is: that all of that hurt and pain *can* be worked through, forgiven, refreshed and renewed through Christ Jesus, Who can make all things new. When we come to terms with how hurtful our disorder may have been on those who love us, it can cause us a lot of grief and pain. When this happens we have to remember it's important to work through feelings, to work through the pain and make amends – to take full responsibility for our actions, to never use our mood disorder and mental health issues as an excuse for our behavior, because no matter what, we're still responsible for our behavior. However, it is important to also remember that the mood disorder isn't something we invited into our lives. Unlike alcoholism or drug addiction, we didn't even open the door to let it in.

Now, as I said earlier in this chapter, your love for the sake of those around you can serve as a real motivation for getting better. Whether it's because of your children, your spouse, your close friends, a partner, or for the sake of future friendships – those people can serve as the motivation. Sometimes we can't do it for ourselves, but we can do it for others, and the best gift you can give to them is to get better. The best thing that you can do is to overcome and begin to not only manage your disorder, but also implement a wellness plan in your life. One of the best ways to begin to make amends with them is to get better – to show them that you are going to do what it takes to have a better life, because if you have a better life and if you successfully manage your disorder, *they're* going to have a better life. They're going to be happier also, and your relationships are going to be better.

Making amends with those whom you have hurt also brings about healing and hope within yourself. When you do that it fills you with newness and a refreshing feeling. When people make amends and are forgiven, relationships have the potential to become much deeper and much more meaningful than before.

Relationships are fraught with conflict. Conflict is not inherently bad; it's what you do with it that matters. If we work through conflict there is a reward. Many of us are task-oriented people. But the reality is we were created for community. That's how God made us. We were created to need one another. The words "one another" appear over 57 times in the Bible, describing how we should treat others: love one another, pray for one another, etc. (See Appendix A.) These passages tell us that we need each other. Because of that, when there's conflict and it's unresolved, life doesn't feel right. We're disconnected and don't enjoy it. So making amends with those we've hurt and taking responsibility for our behavior is key to helping restore the community and harmony that God intends for us.

A change takes place as relationships are restored and mood disorders are successfully treated. A sense of interdependence comes into existence. This refers to the realization that while each person has his own autonomy and freedom, there is also a conscious choice to seek outcomes that are best not only for one's self, but for the relationship as a whole. Interdependence can lead to synergies or outcomes that are better than the sum of outcomes that could be achieved by each individual person. In contrast, and at opposite extremes, unhealthy relationships tend to have tendencies towards enmeshment (few if any personal boundaries) on the one hand or detachment on the other. Enmeshment refers to relationships that are so intertwined that neither person has his/her own sense of identity. Detachment occurs when people isolate themselves from one another to the point that the relationship barely exists. Interdependence is found in the space between enmeshment and detachment.

Early on in my recovery process, when I was beginning to understand that I needed to take responsibility, I did something really stupid. I asked to see somebody that I really hurt. We met and my wife was there with me. I said that I was very sorry and asked for forgiveness from the person I had hurt. Then I said, "But please let me explain 'why' I did it." I said, "Would you please forgive me for doing this-and-thus, but if you just understand why I did it…" Both my wife and this person said, "But now you're trying to excuse your behavior!" At the time I didn't get it. Now I get it. Now I understand. There was no excuse for what I did. The person I had hurt so deeply did not need to understand "why" (my justification for what I had done). Simply put: no matter what my reasoning for doing what I had done that hurt them, I shouldn't have done it. There was no excuse; I was wrong. Taking responsibility for what we've done is key in making amends. There may be an *explanation* for our actions. But that explanation cannot become an *excuse* for bad or inappropriate behavior.

I will never forget the powerful healing between my daughter and me. When I relapsed seven years after my major episode, my daughter was in high school, and it was a great toll on our relationship. It took us many years to rebuild our relationship, but thankfully we did. The night of her wedding, when it was time for the father-daughter dance, we were dancing and I whispered in her ear, "I'm sorry I wasn't a better father. Please forgive me for all my failures and shortcomings and all the times that I failed you, and I pray that I am doing better now and will do better in the future." She looked at me with tears in her eyes and said, "Dad, I haven't cried all day, and now I'm crying. I love you. It's all forgiven." Right then and there, with just the two of us on that dance floor at her wedding reception, a gigantic burden lifted off my shoulders. Once again I heard her say it and once again there was more mending in the relationship.

The bottom line is that when all is said and done, there are no U-Hauls behind a hearse. You really can't take anything along with you to heaven – except for your relationships. Those relationships can go on into eternity. You can leave a legacy of God's redemption in your life to your loved ones, to your children, to your grandchildren and great grandchildren, and for the generations that follow. It doesn't have to be a story about, "Oh, my grandfather was bipolar, and boy, he had this and he was in the hospital, and he did this. . . " It can be about, "My grandfather struggled with bipolar but he *overcame* bipolar." It can be a story about God's redemption in your life and the greatest gift you give to your family and friends, how to overcome difficulties. That's the kind of amends you can make for generations to come. Instead of being about us it becomes being about Him, about God, and His redemption of our broken lives and broken relationships. The focus becomes on Him. It becomes about the power to get back up and to go on because He gives us new starts, fresh beginnings. He gives us Fresh Hope.

When I fell in ministry in 1995, one of my colleagues on the staff, in a congregational meeting, said that I had not finished well. Interestingly enough, he considered that "my finish." In my thinking I wasn't finished, I was 37 years old. You're only finished if you stop and you don't get back up. I didn't consider that an option. I knew I was going to get back up no matter what it took. You see, if you believe that you're through, then you kind of go to the sidelines, sit down, and you wait for the game to be finished. Or, you can get back up and stay in the game of life.

I believe God has a purpose for every single one of us. I believe, mood disorder or no mood disorder, the Lord has given us a purpose. He has a purpose for you, and it's a good purpose. He has a plan for your life and it's a plan to prosper you (Jeremiah 29:11). He's called you to be His child, to live for Him. And that plan and that purpose is carried out for the kingdom of God, and it has to do with the relationships you have with other people and the opportunity to grow His kingdom and share His love with others. And part of the witness and the testimony and the purpose of your life is to show how in spite of the difficulties you face, given your set of circumstances, including a mood disorder and whatever else you have going on in your life, that God is bigger than all of these things and He's made you more than a conqueror - a conqueror who can make amends in relationships.

My two little grandchildren make me the happiest man in the whole world. I know that had it not been for my wife, my two children, my parents, my sister and brother in law, my close friends, extended family and friends, I wouldn't have felt motivated to come so far. Sometimes because of them, and only because of them, I was motivated to get better. I did it for them because many days I couldn't even do it for myself. I did it for them, and gradually I saw the worth in doing it even for myself. Today I praise God for all those relationships.

Matthew 5:23-24 says, "Therefore, if you are offering your gift at the altar and there remember that your brother has something against you, leave your gift there in front of the altar. First go and be reconciled to your brother; then come and offer your gift."

It is time to make amends on your part and let the Lord bring healing and restoration to all broken relationships. It's all part of healing, wellness, and God's redemption in your life.

Consider now how your actions have affected some of your relationships. In the first blank, list a person with whom you have a significant relationship (such as your spouse, parents, children, friends, co-workers). Then describe the ways your actions have affected the relationship. Remember, the point is to accept responsibility for your actions that have hurt your loved ones, not to make excuses for your behavior.

Person: _____

Actions that hurt:_____

_____

_____

_____

_____

_____

_____

Person: _____

Actions that hurt:_____

_____

_____

_____

_____

_____

Person: _____

Actions that hurt:_____

_____

_____

_____

_____

_____

_____

Person: _____

Actions that hurt:_____

_____

_____

_____

_____

_____

Use the space below to write out an apology that addresses the actions you described on the previous pages:

_____

_____

_____

_____

_____

_____

_____

_____

After you have written out the apology, you may find it useful to share it with someone such as a pastor, counselor, or peer support specialist who can help you prepare to deliver the apology in person.

After this first apology, you should repeat this process for each of the actions that hurt the people you listed on the previous pages. You may find it easier to focus on one person at a time, starting with your closest relationships first. Remember, each time you make amends, you will find healing and strength through God's grace.

Key Thoughts

- Messy relationships are common for those of us who have mood disorders.
- God desires that we live together in harmony.
- With treatment and a wellness plan in place you can overcome the symptoms of your mood disorder, and broken relationships can be healed.
- God calls us to be in relationships with others – and we can use this as motivation for our recovery.
- Getting healthy allows us to more fully experience the types of relationships that God intends for us to have.
- Achieving lasting recovery can help establish a "legacy of overcoming" that can affect the lives of future generations.

Section 5

Making Tenet II Personal

Consider what the words of Tenet 2 mean to you personally. In the exercise below, rewrite Tenet 2 to reflect your own life situation. Be as specific as you can.

For example:

Fresh Hope Tenet II

My mood disorder has also affected my relationships and the lives of those around me. Therefore, I choose to overcome for both my own good, and the good of those who love me.

John's Tenet II

While I have been depressed, I have often isolated myself and ignored the needs of others. This has led to pain for me and my loved ones. Because I want to help bring about healing and lasting change, I choose the help and support of Dr. Shaw and Fresh Hope. I will seek reconciliation by taking responsibility for those things that have hurt my loved ones, asking for forgiveness when possible, and choosing to overcome for my own good and for the good of those who love me.

My Tenet II

_____

_____

_____

_____

_____

_____

_____

_____

_____

_____

_____

_____

Every time you read Tenet II, remember your words and mark in your mind that you have worked through and made this commitment.

Q & A with the Psychiatrist

1. How do I draw the distinction between my mood disorder and ordinary emotions?

    Dr. Egger: Generally persistence, intensity and disruption of daily life are the points of differentiation. A sense of sadness or a sense of loss over a bad event such as someone's death or loss of a job is really quite normal. If the symptoms persist unchanged for more than two weeks, in particularly, a sense of depression accompanied by disturbance of sleep or appetite, then we consider this to represent a major depressive episode. Another point of difference is connection to an identifiable event. Brief emotional response to bad life experiences is quite normal. Typically, biochemical mood disorders will tend to worsen unrelated to outside events. Also, the event that seems to be connected, if any, whether the current episode is recent or extremely remote, must be considered.

2. How much can people really change? Aren't our brains sort of hard-wired after a certain age?

    Dr. Egger: No, recent medical evidence points to lifelong tissue regeneration which slows as we age. Besides, what needs to change is the attitude toward how we are living our lives, rather the chemistry of the brain. We are responsible for that attitude.

3.   How do I know when I'm "ready" to make amends?

Dr. Egger: You need to start when you understand the hurts you have caused and upon whom you have inflicted them. You need to start before you are ready. "Ready" becomes a feeling, and making amends is really a decision. Usually the process of making the amends starts well before the individual feels really "ready" and that is more of a response to the decision. Waiting until one "feels ready" rarely produces the decision.

CHAPTER THREE

Pushing Through

TENET III

My disorder can become an excuse. Therefore, I choose to believe I can live a full and rich life in spite of my disorder. I choose the support of people who will urge me to "push through."

Together we do better than trying on our own. We will hold one another accountable for learning, growing, and choosing to push through in hope.

"Therefore, encourage one another and build each other up."
1 Thessalonians 5:11 (NIV)

Section 1
Excuses, Excuses
Why We Make Excuses

Section 2
Choosing to Believe…
…You Can Have a Full and Rich Life

Section 3
Choosing the Support of Others
Prayer and Pushing Through

Section 4

What Does it Mean to Push Through?

How Do You Push Through?

Changing Your Thinking to Help Push Through

Section 5

What's Really Holding You Back?

Section 6

Making Tenet III Personal

Wrap Up

Q & A with the Psychiatrist

Section 1

Excuses, Excuses…

I usually think of excuses as "partial truths" that I use to explain why I did (or didn't do) something. For example, I might say that I was late for an appointment because I had to wait for a train. Well, I did wait at an intersection for about 3 minutes until the train finished going by; but the train didn't make me late. The rest of the truth is that I knew I had to cross the train tracks and there was a possibility of having to wait for a train. I simply didn't leave early enough or allow sufficient time to arrive on time for my appointment. So using the train as an excuse is a partial truth. And a partial truth is an untruth; a lie. While this might seem like a relatively harmless example, it helps set the stage for something far more dangerous – using a mood disorder as an excuse for giving up and refusing to believe you can push through to overcome your symptoms and achieve a lasting recovery.

Why We Make Excuses

I think excuses are so appealing to us because excuses allow us to seemingly transfer blame from ourselves to someone or something else. Other times, we may try to share the blame with others who don't deserve it so we don't feel alone in our wrongdoing. In the first Biblical account of an excuse given by a human, Adam attempted to transfer a share of the blame to both God and Eve when he said, "The woman *you* put here with me – *she* gave me some fruit from the tree" (emphasis added). So if you have ever made an excuse or tried to transfer blame to others, you're not the first person to do it; but please don't use that as an excuse for making excuses!

While some excuses may seem harmless or even humorous, using a mood disorder as an excuse to resist helpful changes can be very harmful to you and everyone around you. It will cause you to move backward instead of moving forward. It won't even keep you where you're at now. Using your mood disorder to avoid the hard work it takes to recover, like other excuses and lies, can lead to feelings of despair and helplessness. It can lead to a false belief that you can no longer live a full and rich life. It can perpetuate or worsen a depressed state, which strengthens negative feelings.

There is something else at work, too. There is evil in this world. St. Paul tells us,

> [21] *"So I find this law at work: Although I want to do good, evil is right there with me.* [22] *For in my inner being I delight in God's law;* [23] *but I see another law at work in me, waging war against the law of my mind and making me a prisoner of the law of sin at work within me.* [24] *What a wretched man I am! Who will rescue me from this body that is subject to death?* [25] ***Thanks be to God, Who delivers me through Jesus Christ our Lord!"*** *(emphasis added)*

So when you fail, as you will from time to time, you need to remember that you're not perfect. Then get up, ask for forgiveness, make amends, and move on! We can expect to struggle, as Paul did. But we know that's not the end of the story. Remember, evil is in the world, but God delivers those who place their hope and faith in Jesus Christ as their Lord and Savior. I find that very encouraging. Do you?

Believing you can live a full and rich life in spite of your disorder is a critical part of recovery and wellness. But there is a risk. What if you're wrong? What if you get your hopes up, then try and fail? Those questions can bring about fears and other feelings that are real and worth discussing with your loved ones, peer support specialist, or therapist. As you do, you should also ask, "What if I could have a full and rich life but instead choose to use my mood disorder as an excuse?" Wouldn't that be far worse?

The truth is that people with mood disorders *can* have a full and rich life. But it takes work. Sometimes you won't feel up to the challenge and that can cause a feeling of self-pity. Don't give in. The hard work is worth it! Believe it or not, the pain that it takes to make healthy changes is less than the pain that comes with staying the same and going backward. This can be a very motivating truth. Accepting the lesser of two pains <u>and</u> achieving the joy that comes with a full and rich life *is* worth the effort. I've been there, and I know it's true.

Author M. Scott Peck states it in this way, "The truth is that our finest moments are most likely to occur when we are feeling deeply uncomfortable, unhappy, or unfulfilled. For it is only in such moments, propelled by our discomfort, that we are likely to step out of our ruts and start searching for different ways or truer answers."

Were any of the challenges listed above excuses based on partial truths? Describe.

_____

_____

_____

_____

_____

Were/are there other excuses that were/are holding you back from recovery and believing that you can live a full and rich life?

_____

_____

_____

_____

_____

Section 2

Choosing to Believe…

Believe. It's a powerful word with several meanings. I've adapted a few definitions from Webster's Dictionary.

Believe (verb):

1. To accept something as true, genuine, or real: "I believe that I and others with mood disorders can live full and rich lives."
2. To accept the word or evidence of someone: "I believe you."
3. To have a firm religious faith: "I believe that Jesus Christ is my Savior and I will live with Him in heaven someday."

…You Can Have a Full and Rich Life

Do you believe that you can have a full and rich life? At times you may find it difficult to envision yourself living a full and rich life in spite of your disorder. During those times, it may be helpful to recall a time when you were genuinely happy. Recall the things that brought joy to your life. What did you enjoy doing and how did you spend your time? These memories may provide a glimpse of what to expect as you recover.

If you are experiencing major depression (or even a mild depressive episode), it may take some extra work to recall good memories. First, you should pat yourself on the back for reading this far. Great job! Then, to recall some good memories, it may be helpful to ask a loved one to help you recall some of your memories from a more healthy time.

It's important to envision a full and rich life because it can serve as a powerful motivator for you to work on your recovery. It will encourage you as you push through during the difficult times.

Visualize yourself living a full and rich life. Describe what that looks like to you.

_____

_____

_____

_____

Describe a time when it seemed difficult to believe that you could live a full and rich life in spite of your disorder. How did you feel?

_____

_____

_____

_____

What were some of the challenges that you were facing when it seemed difficult to believe that you could live a full and rich life in spite of your disorder?

_____

_____

_____

_____

_____

_____

Section 3

Choosing the Support of Others

Having a friend who will encourage you and give you a friendly little nudge or a great big push can make a big difference. You've probably heard the saying "misery loves company." While there is a lot of truth to that saying, having a close friend who will help you push through during the difficult times is something that you won't always appreciate, much less love. But keep this in mind: company doesn't love misery. So if you have a friend who sticks with you during the difficult times and urges you to push through, it's a blessing. If you don't, you might find encouragement from a counselor, support group, or peer support specialist.

Not long ago, I had a friend who was going through a very serious bout of major depression. Having been through a mental health diagnosis and working through my recovery, I felt that I was very knowledgeable about treatments for depression. I called my friend on a regular basis and did a lot of listening because I really cared about him and what he was going through.

I believed that there were some things he needed to question. I challenged "Joe" in regards to some of his thinking and where he was getting some of his information. I questioned the wisdom of talking to his pain doctor about his depression and getting medicine from this pain doctor instead of going to a psychiatrist.

At that point Joe said that he needed to back away from his friendship with me. He made it clear to me that he really just wanted me to listen. He really did not want me to be challenging him to change or "push through." And the truth is, he didn't want a friend who was going to encourage him to move toward wellness. But the fact remains, "If it doesn't challenge you, it doesn't change you."

I don't consider someone who doesn't challenge me and encourage me to be a good friend. In fact, my definition of friendship includes somebody who loves me enough *to* challenge me when my thinking is off track, or when my behavior is off track. A true friend doesn't just listen and hear me, but he/she understands me and sometimes helps me see things a different way. It's too easy in our pain to want to find people that will "just listen" and have pity on us; listening to our excuses while we wallow away in unhealthy mindsets. It's too easy to want friends who do not challenge us to push through our pain so that we can live a full life. Why? Because frankly, it's not what we want to hear when we are wrapped up in our own self-pity. And it's so easy to get stuck in that mode. It's easy because our thinking is so distorted because our brain chemistry is so off. And so, we get stuck wallowing and not pushing through.

We need people who love us and care about us to urge us to push through. Therefore, be careful who you choose as your friends. It has been said that we become like those who are closest to us. So, choose carefully. Negativity does not breed wellness. It simply fertilizes one's self-pity. Our negativity can easily cause us to believe that things will never change; that we can't get better. Well, don't always believe what you think! It's dangerous.

You and I need to choose to believe that we can live full and rich lives *in spite* of our disorders. We have to say to ourselves that even if our excuses are legitimate, we're just not going to use any of those excuses. We're going to do whatever it takes to get better.

One of the best things you can do in order to push through is to have safe people around you who are going to challenge you to push through. One of the most important things my counselor taught me very early on in my recovery process was the fact that if airplane pilots never learn to fly by the dashboard instruments of the plane, they can never fly totally safe, and certainly can't fly at nighttime. That's because without learning how to trust the instruments on the dashboard and only trusting their "instincts" they run the risk of experiencing vertigo. And vertigo might cause them to believe they're going up when actually they're going down. Or they might feel like they're going down when they're actually going up. And that's what happens to you and me emotionally—especially with a mood disorder. We can get all goofed up in our feelings and our thinking. So, we need trusted people to be our "dashboard instruments," which help us avoid vertigo, if you will: those three to five people who are very safe for us and who are going to be our instruments that we're going to trust in spite of how we feel or how we might be thinking.

John Kennedy, Jr. died in a plane crash because of vertigo, most likely. He was flying at night and he did not know how to fly by reading the instruments. He did it by sight, and therefore he was not reading the instruments. And without using the instruments, a pilot is not as safe as he could be normally with the proper training. And the same is true for you and me. We need that dashboard, that group of people who are safe.

Now, taking it a step further, I would say that the best thing you and I could do in order to really make sure that we push through is to put ourselves smack dab in the center of a circle of accountability. In that circle of accountability you might have your doctor, your spouse, your counselor, your close friend or two, and maybe even a small accountability group. These people all can talk to one another and they can talk to you. In other words, your doctor and your counselor and your pastor and your friend and your spouse – they can all talk to each other. You'll need to sign waivers of confidentiality for your doctor to be able to talk to your pastor, and for your pastor to be able to talk to your doctor. This helps to open lines of communication that will provide accountability for you. And they are going to be encouraging you to push through. Another idea that helps is peer support. Those of us who have been through the recovery process have a way of helping one another that other people can't necessarily do when they haven't had mood disorders. It's one of those things where once you've been through it you know kind of what things "smell" like along the way.

We can tell what's going on with one another at times and call each other out, help each other and encourage one another, and be positive with each other. And peer support is extremely helpful in guiding us forward and pushing us through the difficulties and the challenges.

Since 2001 I have continued to meet with my "dashboard instruments" twice a month. Those "instruments" are three men who are fellow pastors whom I trust, love me as their brother, and ask me a lot of tough questions. They pry. They challenge my thinking. They hold me accountable. They listen. They care. They weep with me. They laugh with me. They pray with me and for me. My wife can talk to them at any time if she is not able to "get" me to understand any concerns she might have, and they have full access to my doctor. But, most of all, they challenge me constantly to move forward; to live well. They are my circle of accountability.

Prayer and Pushing Through

Pushing through in prayer is one of the best things you and I can do in order to push through in our recovery. You need personal prayer warriors. Seek out folks who take prayer very seriously and ask them to become a warrior for you.

Some time ago I came across an acronym for PUSH regarding prayer, and it goes like this: **P**ray **U**ntil **S**omething **H**appens – P.U.S.H. And I'd like you to think of this as you push through and you P.U.S.H. In other words, you push through and you keep going until something happens. And you keep praying until something happens. The Lord is there with us. He's there with you. And He wants to help you. He is for you. As you pray, He's going to give you the strength you need. He's not going to leave you. He has not forsaken you, nor will He forsake you. He loves you, and He wants to see you succeed. He's got a great plan for you!

My manic episode resulted in separation from my church, causing great pain to my family, congregation, and me. I prayed for healing, closure, and reconciliation. I kept praying – for weeks, for month, for years. As the months passed, I experienced times of great frustration with God and others, but I also trusted that God had a plan. And He did. It took *seventeen years*, but it has unfolded in a way that only the Lord can do; in a way that I would have never thought of or could have imagined. There's been healing, reconciliation, and redemption. And the Lord gets all of the glory! Whether or not any reconciliation would have ever happened, I had to push through in prayer and push through in forgiveness. Had I not remained faithful in prayer and continued to push through, I could have become bitter and self-absorbed in my hurt. When we hold on to unforgiveness toward someone and we don't forgive – it's like us drinking poison but expecting the other person to die!

So a large part of pushing through is prayer. We need to push through, spiritually and emotionally. Don't stop praying. Pray until something happens. And press on until something happens.

List some safe people you could ask to become part of a circle of accountability for you:

_____

_____

_____

_____

_____

If you receive advice that you don't like from someone on the list above, what will you do?

_____

_____

_____

_____

How would you like these people to pray for you?

_____

_____

_____

_____

_____

Write out a prayer that expresses your desire to push through:

_____

_____

_____

_____

_____

Section 4

What Does it Mean to Push Through?

It means that you simply won't use any excuses that hinder your recovery. It means that you're going to push through and you're going to insist on being the best you possibly can be with where you're at today, no matter what. It means that no matter who's told you what, you're not going to remain where you're at; you *expect* to get better to the point that you are no longer experiencing the daily effects of your disorder, and you are successfully managing and enjoying your life rather than letting your disorder manage you. That's going to vary from person to person. But it means that you don't give up, and you don't give in to the disorder, and you feel as though you *will* conquer it and *will* be victorious over it.

Pushing through is something you do one day at a time, doing the best and being the best that you can be emotionally. It means that you choose a positive, faith-filled outlook and attitude regarding your life every single day. Noted theologian Karl Barth stated it so well: "Courage is fear that has said its prayers." It means that you celebrate the victories, even the smallest little victories. It also means you learn to laugh at yourself; that you see your failures as opportunities to grow and learn. It means that you see any failure as being nothing more than a stepping-stone to success. It also means that you do not always trust your feelings or what you think. Certainly our feelings, moods, and thinking can mislead us. So, you stay focused on the discipline to see the goal ahead. And you forget what lies behind you, like Paul says; using those "instruments" on your dashboard (your circle of accountability) to avoid vertigo. Don't fear change. Change fear.

You make sure you surround yourself with people that love you, and are going to be encouraging people to you. You confess the word of God into your life situation.

How Do You Push Through?

Now, it's important to realize that 'pushing through' is a process. Seldom does it happen like somebody flicking a light switch on. It's more like a s-l-o-w dimmer switch. It happens day by day, and it happens moment by moment, and it's something you have to keep on doing. Some days are easier than others. But it's also a mindset that says, "I am not going to settle for less than the best that my life can be. I am going to live well."

Sometimes therapists and doctors will tell you, "Well, this is probably going to be the best it can be," because they don't want us to live in frustration or want us to be disappointed. But here's where faith comes in. Here's where God comes in. Sometimes, medicine can do only so much. Sometimes therapy can only do so much. We are people of faith, and our God is quite able. In Mark chapter 9, the disciples bring a man to Jesus who's very demonized, and they can't do

Our God is quite able

anything with him. They've tried and tried, and the father says, "Jesus, if You can do anything," and Jesus looks at the father and says, "What do you mean IF I can do anything? With God, all things are possible."

This is where that decision of hope, the decision of faith, knowing that the doctor may say "this is as good as it's going to get," we still look to God for even more complete healing and things that are better. No different than the woman who has rheumatoid arthritis, or the person who has fibromyalgia, or the person who has cancer, or the person who has any kind of serious illness: even if the doctor says, "This is as good as it's going to be" or "This is it now. This is all I can do medically." Fine. But our God can do infinitely more.

This is also where you and I can really encourage one another. It's so unreal what people of faith can do for one another, even what people of faith can do for those who have very little, if any, faith. Remind yourself, "I am strong, because I've been weak. I am fearless, because I've been afraid. I am wise, because I've been foolish."

Pushing through is an attitude – a faith attitude that says, "I WILL get through this." The kind of attitude that says, "I'm going through hell, but I'm not going to stop. I am going to keep movin' forward!" Because when you're going through hell, you don't stop! And when you're catchin' hell, you don't hold it! It's the kind of thing where you and I say, "I <u>will</u> <u>not</u> let this do me in, nor will I become my diagnosis. And I <u>will</u> enjoy a rich and full life *in spite* of having bipolar disorder, or depression, or whatever the case may be. And I'm not going to use any excuses, and I'm not going to wallow in self-pity about it. 'Cause there's worse things I could have; there's much worse things I could have gone through. And I'm going to make sure that I listen to the people around me, people who support me and love me, and who are going to challenge me and encourage me to push through and get better every day. That's what it means to "push through."

You develop an attitude of knowing that you will just take it one day at a time, one hour at a time, one moment at a time, one situation at a time. And if you slip backwards, you don't let it take you completely down the drain! So you slip up, so you go backwards, so you have a few moments, so you have a bad day – so you have a couple of bad days emotionally. These instances do not define the rest of your life!

That reminds me of the story of the woman who was in front of me at Weight Watchers® many years ago, who began to cry as she was on the scale and confessed she had eaten some M & Ms. The lady weighing her said, "Oh, my, how many did you eat?"

She said, "Oh, I ate probably 10 or 12."

And the lady at the scale said, "Oh, and how many would you have normally eaten?"

The woman said, "Well, I would have eaten a large bag of them!"

She said, "Well, you made progress!"

And the lady kept crying and wailed, "No, I didn't. I ate 10 or 12 of them!"

And she said, "Well, what color were they?" trying to help her lighten up and understand that you've got to celebrate the victory. "If you would have eaten the whole bag, but you only ate 10 or 12, that's better than eating the whole bag."

So you have a bad day. Okay. That's better than having a whole bad week or a whole bad month. Maybe you gave in and you weren't able. Maybe you used a whole bunch of excuses, and you realize it, and you did it for a couple of days. But that's better than a couple of weeks, or a couple of months, or a couple of years of excuses.

When you fail at pushing through, you simply get back up and keep pushing. It's just that simple. It is not necessarily easy. But, it's certainly not complicated.

Changing Your Thinking to Help Push Through

Learning to push through is learning to change your thinking. When you can change your thinking it will change, to a certain degree, how you feel. And it will even change your mood. Also it means that you and I have to learn how to talk with others about what's going on inside of us. We have to process our emotions and feelings in healthy ways. Instead of keeping them inward and letting them rule how we feel and how we act, how about us talking about them? Like Paul says, let's focus our attention and take captive our thinking by focusing our thoughts on the helpful things, the positive things, the things filled with faith.

> "*⁴ Rejoice in the Lord always. I will say it again: Rejoice! ⁵ Let your gentleness be evident to all. The Lord is near. ⁶ Do not be anxious about anything, but in every situation, by prayer and petition, with thanksgiving, present your requests to God. ⁸ Finally, brothers and sisters, whatever is true, whatever is noble, whatever is right, whatever is pure,*

whatever is lovely, whatever is admirable—if anything is excellent or praiseworthy—think about such things. [9] Whatever you have learned or received or heard from me, or seen in me—put it into practice. And the God of peace will be with you." Philippians 4: 4-6, 8-9

Another thing that enables us to push through is to purge ourselves of negative self-talk. We all have self-talk. We all talk about ourselves in our thinking. What do we say about ourselves? What do you say about yourself inside your head? "I'm stupid." "I should have thought of this." "I shouldn't have done that, or "I always…" and "I never…" What do you say? And how much negative is there that you say about yourself? It's interesting to pay attention to that. Get rid of as much of that as possible. Work on it. Because it helps in pushing through when you can get rid of those thoughts.

Doing simple things that help maintain your mood, like sleeping, eating, exercising, setting a routine – will help you in thinking more clearly and less negatively. Begin to identify the negating lies you believe and are at the basis of so much of your emotional pain. When you get to those core negative beliefs or lies, it will begin to set you free to heal emotionally and bring about positive, faith-filled thinking.

What are some failures you can't seem to forgive yourself? As you PUSH and pray through each, what will you ask God to make happen instead?

_____

_____

_____

_____

List 3-5 statements of negative self-talk that you want to ask God to help you take captive.

_____

_____

_____

_____

_____

_____

_____

Name some small hurdles you have pushed through to celebrate a victory. Complete these statements.

I used to _____

_____

Now I _____

_____

I used to _____

_____

Now I _____

_____

Section 5

What's Really Holding You Back?

There are a lot of things that can hold you back from getting better. Here are some of the most common traps:

1. Excuses—They will cause you to move backwards. They won't even keep you where you are. Excuses can quickly cause you to lose hope and believe that you can no longer live a full and rich life. Don't buy into those lies!

2. Self-pity—Too much focus on self. And that usually happens with mood disorders. We become so focused on ourselves. Mood disorders are very demanding things.

3. Lack of Discipline and Will—Wanting our mood disorders to be over with now, and not seeing pushing through as a day by day, step by step process.

4. Lack of Forgiveness—Especially of one's own self, can hold us back.

5. Lack of Patience—Impatient with ourselves at not being able to push through, impatient for the mood to be over with, or tired of waiting for the depression to lift. Sometimes patience is more important than even your discipline or self-will.

6. Not Having the Right Medical Care—It's important to work with a psychiatrist and therapist who take time to listen to you and regularly assess your treatment plan.

7. Surrounding Yourself with People Who are Enablers—Enablers are those people who allow you to think your thoughts and behaviors are normal. We sometimes need accountability, someone to say, "Hey! Wait a minute. Your behavior or your thinking is inappropriate."

8. No Encouragers or Support System—Sometimes we truly don't have anyone positive who is there for us. Nobody saying, "I know you can do this. I know you can do this. It's going to be OK." Sometimes it's because we don't have anybody else we know who ever made it through. That's why peer support, in a setting like Fresh Hope, is so important. It's in groups like this that we see other people who have made it through things that we're going through. And we see how well they're doing and the insights they have, and then that encourages us.

What are some of the things that have held you back?

_____

_____

_____

_____

Describe how you can overcome these challenges:

_____

_____

_____

_____

Key Thoughts

- Don't make excuses for your failures. Sin is in the world, and everyone makes mistakes.
- You can life a full and rich life *in spite* of your disorder. This is a critical part of recovery and wellness.
- The hard work of recovery is worth it. Don't give up.
- Envision a rich and full life to help you push through the difficult times.
- Choose a circle of accountability of people who are safe, who will be truthful, and will challenge you to push through.
- Prayer is key in your recovery.
- Recovery is a process; rejoice at the successes and push through the setbacks.
- Get rid of negative self talk.

Section 6

Making Tenet III Personal

Consider what the words of Tenet III mean to you personally. In the exercise below, rewrite Tenet III to reflect your own life situation. Be as specific as you can.

Fresh Hope Tenet III

My disorder can become an excuse. Therefore, I choose to believe I can live a full and rich life in spite of my disorder. I choose the support of people who will urge me to "push through."

John's Tenet III

While I have been depressed, I have often given up and given in, using my condition as an excuse to avoid things that seem difficult. However, I realize that there is a richness and fullness in life that I haven't fully experienced in a long time. I choose to believe that this fullness and richness will be restored to me. Because I want to help bring about healing and lasting change, I choose the help and support of Dr. Shaw, Fresh Hope, and my spouse. I will ask them to urge to me to push through and I will listen to them when they encourage me.

My Tenet III

_____

_____

_____

_____

_____

_____

_____

_____

Every time you read Tenet III, remember these words you have written and your resolve to live a full life *in spite* of your disorder.

Q & A with the Psychiatrist

1. Can I have my spouse, pastor, and/or other accountability partners contact my doctor directly if they are concerned about me? What type of release form do you suggest?

    Dr. Egger: Yes, each must have individual release forms on file at their physician's, physiatrist's or therapist's office. Each provider will have a standard release form.

2. Are there exercises I can do on my own and/or with my support group to help me correct faulty thinking when I am discouraged?

    Dr. Egger: When perceiving discouragement, start jotting down the thoughts occurring and then rank them in order from most to least frequent. After preparing the list, read 1 Peter 5:7 and place your cares upon the Lord, Philippians 4:6-8.

    When sensing you're not making progress reaching joy, you need to present it to three accountability partners, either together or alone, and have them list their observations. Then ask them for ways to move beyond that particular observation or behavior. This needs to be highly specific.

3. How can I move past the things that are holding me back?

    Dr. Egger: After completing the rank order as noted above, pray over it and then present it preferably to two or more of your accountability partners. After that, daily speak aloud that these obstacles are overcome because we are "more than conquerors in Christ Jesus" and that because of God they are past and overcome.

CHAPTER 4

There's Hope

TENET IV

My disorder can lead me to feel hopeless. Therefore, I choose to believe, regardless of my feelings, that there is help and hope for my physical, emotional, psychological and spiritual well-being.

Together we remind each other that our hope and joy come from the Lord. He alone is able to fulfill our needs in every aspect of our lives.

"For I know the plans I have for you, declares the LORD, plans to prosper you and not to harm you, plans to give you hope and a future."
Jeremiah 29:11 (NIV)

Section 1
Choose Hope

Section 2
How Does Hopelessness Happen?

Section 3
How Does Hope Happen?

Section 4
Making Tenet IV Personal

Wrap Up
Q & A with the Psychiatrist

Section 1

Choose Hope

T he fourth tenet of Fresh Hope might be considered the "core tenet" because it deals with the issue of choosing hope in spite of feeling hopeless. Choosing hope and choosing to be hopeful in spite of feeling hopeless is a key concept within the Fresh Hope tenets.

The word "hope" can very easily be misunderstood, because when the word is used it has various meanings. For example, if I said to you, "I sure hope that everything works out for you." I would be saying that I am "wishful," joining with you in wishing/hoping that things will work out well. But if I were to say to you, "Things certainly are very bleak for you right now and I don't know how it will all turn out, but I know that your hope is in the Lord and that will get you through everything." In this example, I am talking about a different type of hope than in the previous sentence. In the first example, I'm "wishing" or joining together with you in your desire for things to work out well. However, in the second example hope is not a "desire" or "wish," but is a statement of faith and fact. It is this type of hope we are talking about in this tenet. In other words, hope that is not a desire, but a certainty. It is a sure and certain hope that all will be well no matter what our circumstances may be at the time. This is what I call "faith-filled" hope. And because of the certainty of faith, we can choose to have this hope *in spite* of how hopeless our circumstances may appear.

Let's say that you have a favorite football team. And your team is scheduled to play in the playoffs. However, you have a required work activity that will keep you from watching the live game, so you record it. When you get home, you sit down in your lazy boy chair to watch the recorded game a few hours after it has ended. You log onto your laptop to check emails while the game plays. Will you look online to see who won the game, or will you wait to watch for the outcome? You and I both know that if you watch the game knowing who wins, verses not knowing, you will have two very different experiences. If you know that your team wins but is behind until the very end of the fourth quarter, you will react very differently as you watch it as opposed to how you might react if you didn't know the ending score. If you know the ending of the game but your team is behind through most of it, you will have a "sure and certain hope" that everything will be OK in the end. But if you watch the game not knowing the outcome, you will have a "strong desire" for it to end well, but it won't be a "for sure" – and will cause you some anxiety – especially because they are so far behind and the game is nearly over! This is the difference with the meaning of the word "hope" that I am talking about in this tenet.

You and I are people of faith. We already know how the "game" or "story" will end. We already know that in spite of how things may appear, all is well because of Christ. For He has already won it for us! We already KNOW that God WILL work all things out together for our good (Romans 8:28). Even when we are in the midst of difficulties and dire circumstances, even though we may feel hopeless, we are able through the strength of the Holy Spirit because of our faith, to *choose* to be hope-filled, because we are certain of the outcome. We have a "sure and certain hope" in Christ Jesus, no matter what!

Now, we remember the job of the Enemy is to get you and me to question the ending. IF he can get you and me to question whether the Lord is really with us or for us then he, the Enemy, can get us to be frustrated, discouraged, and hopeless. And when you and I feel hopeless, we focus instead on our circumstances and lose sight of the sure and certain hope we have in Jesus. We end up feeling hopeless and we begin to believe that we are in fact in a hopeless situation. Yet, the truth has not changed. What is that truth? The truth has not changed: Jesus has won the victory. He is for you. He has promised to be with you *no matter what*.

Let's go back to the previous illustration of watching the recording of a playoff football game. Remember, if you watch it knowing that your team wins, you will experience it a lot differently than if you didn't know your team was going to win. So, if you know that your team wins, you are able to endure your team being behind until the end of the fourth quarter, because you have the confidence that *in spite* of it appearing as though the other team is going to win; you know the ending score. But, let's say one of your so-called "friends" calls you and begins to tell you that you're wrong about knowing that your team wins. The "friend" tells you that it is not true! Your "friend" tells you that your team loses. And you begin to question whether or not your team wins. In fact, as you are watching the game you begin to become discouraged and disillusioned with your team! Yet, while your so-called "friend" has gotten you to question the truth about the end of the game; the truth that your team won the game has NOT changed. And this is exactly what the Enemy, Satan, does with you and me when we face difficult situations in life, not just with mental health issues.

Satan's goal is to get you and me to question the truth about the outcome of the "game." And if he can get us to begin to question it, then our feelings begin to determine what we believe, as opposed to our feelings being based upon the truth in spite of what we see or are experiencing. This is why in Tenet IV we say that we CHOOSE hope in spite of our feelings. Just because we may feel hopeless, that does not change the truth of us having a sure and certain hope in Christ Jesus. Therefore, no matter what our circumstances, we are in fact NEVER without hope. Real hope, hope that is sure, hope that is certain, hope that is based on the truth. It's not the kind of hope that is a "desirous wish"; wishing and desiring that everything will work out but, not knowing that it will or won't for sure. For those of us who believe in Christ Jesus as our Lord and Savior, for those of us who know the true and living God – we are NEVER without hope, even in the worst of circumstances. Even though our whole world may be falling apart around us, we know Who wins! Therefore, we *choose* to find our hope in what is true instead of basing our hope upon our feelings or circumstances.

Hope is an issue of faith. However, choosing it is a process. It's not like flicking on your "hope-switch" and the feelings and frustrations of hopelessness all go away in some magical way. In this tenet we are not saying that you must ignore your feelings or your circumstance. But rather, we are saying that when you are hopeless and feel ing as though there is no hope at all, you must *choose* with your will through faith to remember the truth that, because of Jesus, we are never without hope. He will get you through it and in the end He will work it out for your good. When we choose to believe the truth as opposed to basing what we believe upon our feelings, our feelings will in fact begin to change. What we believe brings about our view of all things and causes us to feel various ways. We are saying, "choose to believe the truth about never

Because of Jesus, we are never without hope

being without hope, and it will begin to change how you feel about your circumstances." It will begin to take you from hope-less to becoming hope-filled. In other words, in the midst of the flood of hopeless-ness, hold fast to the rock-solid, firmly-anchored

hope in Christ, and you will begin to see your circumstances differently. And even if the flood worsens, you will have hope, because once the flood is over – and it will be over at some point – you will be standing on the solid rock of Jesus.

I've heard it said that you can't believe everything you think. It's true. There are a lot of things I might think. But that does not make them true. I'd have to say that the same is true of feelings. Feelings are not necessarily true. Just because you feel something does not mean that it is true. Now, I'm not saying that we should ignore our feelings. Instead, we need to find out what beliefs are driving those feelings. If a belief is not based upon the truth of God's Word, then it's important to start to change our thinking, versus acting upon our feelings. The truth will set you and me free from discouragement and hopelessness.

Please note: this idea of choosing hope is a faith choice. From my perspective you truly can have hope – absolute, sure, and certain hope – with faith in Christ.

And the kind of hope I'm talking about is that "fresh hope" that comes from God. It's a sure hope. It's the kind of hope that we can be absolutely certain of. It's hope that's rooted in knowing that with God all things are possible. It's hope that's rooted in knowing that God loves you, He is for you, and that He will never leave or forsake you. It's hope that is not at all dependent on you, but all dependent on God.

Here's a list of hope-filled statements of fact/truth based upon God's Word that you and I can choose to believe out of faith – even when we are feeling hopeless:

- With God all things are possible.
- God is for me, so who or what can be against me?
- God will not leave nor forsake me.
- God has not given up on me.
- God can redeem my pain.
- I can help others with the same help I've been given.
- God is the source of my hope.
- God can and will redeem my past.
- God loves me unconditionally.
- No matter my circumstances I can have peace and hope.
- The truth sets me free and gives me hope.
- Forgiveness and mercy and grace are His gifts to me.
- Success is built upon failure; when we are weak, He is strong.

You might even want to use this list by reading it daily until hopelessness becomes a distant memory.

Lest you think that I am clueless about the feelings of hopelessness and despair that come about when you are dealing with a persistent and debilitating chronic mental health issue, please know, I have suffered very deep clinical depression, and have felt so hopeless that the only way out of all of the pain that I could see at that point was death itself. I have been suicidal. I've been so low that I could not get out of bed. I have been curled up in the fetal position in the dark more than once. And in those darkest moments when every fiber of my being was screaming in hopelessness, I fought with my entire spiritual might to hold on to Jesus. It was by a very thin frayed thread of faith that I hung onto the hope in Christ. I did NOT feel hopeful at all. I felt suicidal. I felt desperate, discouraged, and hopeless. But I knew that truth was not based upon how I felt. The truth was the truth no matter what, and that truth was that the Lord was with me and He would see me through this violent storm of hopelessness. So, it was with this thin frayed thread of faith, which was most likely even smaller than a mustard seed, I chose to believe there was hope.

And lest you think that I am clueless about the feelings of hopelessness and despair that easily come about as you begin taking steps toward recovery, I also know how frustrating and at times seemingly fruitless those initial days, months, and even years of recovery feel. I remember clearly feeling "flat" and the idea of having to force myself to even get up, and possibly do one or two things, would wear me out. I remember not being able to even make it through the morning hours without a nap. It was so easy to slip into feeling hopeless. Things were not changing quickly or easily. It was such hard work. I didn't know if I could do it. I didn't know if I believed. I didn't know if I really wanted to work that hard. But, I chose to believe what I did not feel. I chose it because of my faith in Christ Jesus. And step-by-step, moment-by-moment, ever-so-slowly things changed. And I began to feel some hope. It was a process. It took time. Quite honestly had it not been for my faith, the Word of God, and those who were around me who were faith-filled encouragers, I would not have made it. I would have given into the feelings of hopelessness and helplessness and either committed suicide or just simply "given-in" to not getting better – and most likely would have gotten sicker.

Identify times you feel most hopeless.

What truths has Satan made you question about your recovery?

_____

_____

_____

_____

What lies is Satan flooding you with? How does it make you feel knowing that you *always* have hope in Christ Jesus, that with God ALL things are possible?

_____

_____

_____

_____

Return to the list of hope-filled statements in this section. Circle the 3-5 you currently most need to remind yourself of. Then write each on a post-it or card and tape to your bathroom mirror. Every time you look in the mirror, read these aloud looking at your reflection.

Section 2

How Does Hopelessness Happen?

Certainly what causes thoughts and feelings of hopelessness are too numerous to cover completely here. However, I'd like to look at what I believe are the primary causes.

Thoughts and feelings of hopelessness easily take over our minds when our brain chemistry is not working properly. And when the brain chemistry is not working properly, our thinking and perceived reality becomes skewed and twisted. Our brain chemistry can cause feelings and thoughts of hopelessness and despair even if there is nothing going on in our lives that would situationally cause such thoughts and feelings.

Thoughts and feelings of hopelessness may also come about when we are in a life crisis and become "stuck" in the pain over an unusual length of time. This in turn changes our brain chemistry, due to the prolonged period of stress and survival mode that a life crisis causes.

The feelings and thoughts of ongoing hopelessness, anxiety and utter "gut-wrenching" desperation are simply debilitating, and left untreated can easily lead to getting even sicker and possibly even death. Hopelessness sucks the life right out of you, to the point where even the simplest things of life are far too hard to do. The emotional pain can become so dramatic and traumatic that it becomes unbearable. Every now and then someone will tell me that they can't imagine ever being that hopeless. I always tell them to thank the Lord that they don't know! I was the same way until it happened to me. You and I both know that the hopelessness that robs you of life is very real.

Of course, it's important to remember, as discussed previously in this chapter, that the Enemy also "messes" with us in trying to get us to doubt that we have a sure and certain hope in Christ Jesus. He plays with our minds, trying to get us to have fear in our situations because they appear so dire and hopeless. The Enemy wants us to forget that God has always been faithful. In fact, right now you might be saying,

"Wait a minute, I'm not so sure that God has been faithful all the time to me!" Well, my friend, that IS hopelessness!

As believers, you and I must understand that Satan attempts to get us off track with our faith in the Lord all the time, whether we have a mood disorder or not. And when someone has a mood disorder, a chemical imbalance in the brain, which affects his/her thinking, it is just a bit easier for the Enemy to hook-into the fears that one might have at that point.

There are those in the Christian community who believe that there is no such thing as "mental illness." They believe that it's all spiritual, and a matter of sin and disbelief. There are also those in the Christian community who believe that mental health issues are strictly physiological, and have removed the element of faith from the equation. The truth is, both extreme points of view are lacking. There is such a thing as brain illness such as depression, bipolar, and anxiety disorders, which are just as much a physical illness as cancer or diabetes. And just like all of life, you can't separate spiritual matters from anything in life. Scripture tells us that the Enemy is always at work, prowling like a lion, looking for those who he can devour (1 Peter 5:8). Anything within our human condition that has to do with illnesses, brokenness, pain, and hurt are all rooted in the brokenness of mankind from the fall into sin. You can't single out mental health issues as "sin issues" separate from something such as heart disease or cancer. In doing so, you are dismissing the fact that the brain is an organ in your body just as any other organ. Your thinking and thought process are in essence a function of an organ with your body. And that organ, just like every other organ in your body, has been affected by the fallen broken state of mankind. People get sick and have diseases because of this brokenness. The Bible tells us that this brokenness is the root cause and reason for pain, hurt, sickness, and death.

While we are on this topic of sin, mental health, faith, and hopelessness – it's important to note here that unlike other physical illnesses and disorders, mental health issues bring with them bad behavior. In fact, sometimes they bring about actual sinful behavior.

For example, an individual who has bipolar disorder may have periods of hyper-sexuality during a manic episode and act out sexually leading to sinful behavior. While the bipolar disorder is at the root of the sinful behavior, it is not an excuse. Mental health issues are part of the human condition, which has come about due to the brokenness of mankind. And at times these mental health conditions, when left untreated, may bring about actual behaviors that are sinful. But of course, the individual is still responsible for any inappropriate or sinful behavior, whether they have a mental health issue or not.

Now, with all of this said, you also need to understand that there is always a spiritual dynamic to mental health issues. We are whole beings: body, soul, and mind. Therefore, when we face physical challenges, we also care for the emotional and spiritual aspects of a person. There is, in fact, a lack of spiritual disciplines in our lives that may contribute to hopelessness and despair. Not caring for ourselves spiritually (not doing the things that help us spiritually) can contribute to our hopelessness. We can give ourselves various types of spiritual care that will help us fight against the hopelessness and bring about hope. The Lord has provided us with "spiritual medicine" in His Word to fight against the thoughts and feelings of hopelessness; yet many times when in the pits of hopelessness, we avoid the "medicine."

So we end up:

- Isolating – not going to worship or not participating in a small prayer or Bible study group where you are encouraged spiritually.
- Not praying – simply because you feel like you can't and have no desire to do so. You also feel like God isn't listening and doesn't care anyway.
- Not going to my support group – again, isolating, cutting myself off from encouragement and hope through the support of others who have "been there".
- Not reading the Bible – because we can't focus and feel like we aren't getting anything out of it.
- Avoiding spiritual people – because they are just going to over-simplify it all and tell us to pray and read the Bible.

- Not being in charge of what we are thinking about – and instead just letting our thoughts continually drag us farther down into the abyss of darkness.

When you and I feel the most hopeless and end up doing/not doing these things for ourselves spiritually, we are then avoiding the very things that might enable us to spiritually fight against hopelessness. When feeling hopeless, it's so easy to excuse ourselves from having to fight for ourselves through spiritual self-care! Why? Because when we are hopeless we feel like we cannot do anything, and that anything we do won't matter anyway. So, we let our feelings dictate what we do. And the truth is that sometimes we simply need to do anything we can to change our feelings of hopelessness. In other words, sometimes we just have to get off of our "spiritual butts" and get up and do spiritual self-care, whether we feel like it or not! In fact, if you don't feel like it, that's when you most need to discipline yourself to do it.

I'll be honest with you: I can be really lazy. For some reason the very things that are in my best interest to do, such as physical or spiritual exercise – which require discipline – I don't like to do. I tend too easily to do things I like to do. And I also prefer to "feel like" doing them prior to doing them. You know what I mean?

Don't get me wrong, I'm a very motivated person about things that I am interested in or that are easy. But, on things that I don't find interesting or think are too mundane, then I don't "feel" like doing them. Honestly, I don't like to do things I don't "feel" like doing! (Oh no! Did I just write that down for everyone to read?) Well, it's the truth.

It is through my recovery that I have been learning discipline. In fact, I think had I been disciplined prior to major episodes in my life, those episodes may have not been as big of factors as they ended up being. I am learning that whether I *feel* like doing something cannot determine whether or not I do it. Instead, I *must* do certain things because these things will bring about feelings of hope, self-worth, and wellness. "The pain of discipline is far less than the pain of regret" (Olympic swimmer Sarah Bombell).

So, instead of:

- Isolating from worship, Bible study, or a prayer group, I need to keep, or start, attending – even if I don't feel like it. Because if it is a healthy and life-giving group, whether I felt like going or not, it will begin to strengthen me. Maybe not right away…but sooner or later it will. (Please note, this is very important: You must get fed spiritually. If the group is judgmental, negative, or non-productive, you must find another group.)

- Not praying, I will pray even if I feel like the Lord isn't there or isn't listening to me. I'll commit myself to doing it daily – and when I feel like I can't do it, I will simply tell Him how I don't feel like praying. I'll tell Him about how awful I feel and how hopeless my life feels – after all, that's what David did in the Psalms. (Hint: telling God how you feel is, in fact, praying!) Sooner or later I know that, based upon my faith, I will begin to cherish this time with Him.

- Avoiding my support group, I will go even when I don't feel well or feel like it. Why? Because I know that they have "been there" and have encouragement for me to keep going.

- Neglecting God's Word, I'll read the Bible even though I am not able to concentrate enough to really comprehend. I don't have to read a lot of it. Just one verse is enough. And instead of just reading the verse, I'm going to memorize it – even though I don't feel like it. Why? Because the Lord uses His word to fill me with faith and His Holy Spirit. And His Spirit, through this faith course, will sooner or later bring about hope once again.

- Cutting myself off from my friends, I will stay in touch with those who are my spiritual encouragers. And if I don't have any, I will find some. Even though spiritual encouragement sounds trite and "cheesy" when I'm feeling hopeless, it's what I need most at those times. And I will do this in spite of not wanting to. Why? Because that spiritual encouragement will speak to my soul, and my soul will begin to inform my mind, and my mind will begin to once again bring about hope in my life.

- Letting my thinking control me, I will attempt to take charge over my thinking. I will take captive my thoughts instead of just letting them come and allowing myself to dwell on things that are not good or helpful (2 Corinthians 10:5). And even when I fail at doing this, I will keep trying to do it in spite of not feeling like I want to do it. Why? Because I know that I have a lot of toxic thinking and need to replace it with what is true, what is good, and what God says. And sooner or later, my thinking will change. And my Godly thinking will even change my brain chemistry. "Without a doubt, my Christianity is the guiding belief of my life. It gives me hope in a world that is often without hope and an anchor in truth and reality. God is my Intelligent Designer, and this level of information flows from the Holy Spirit." (Dr. Caroline Leaf, *Who Switched Off My Brain?*,©2009 p. 115)

Learning discipline can change toxic, hopeless thoughts into a determined will. Select 3 of the 6 hopeless thoughts from the list above that apply to your life, and complete here. Be specific in naming the actions you're willing to take.

Instead of _____ **, I will** _____

_____

Instead of _____ **, I will** _____

_____

Instead of _____ **, I will** _____

_____

Truths

- No one else can do these things for you or me.
- You can't wait until you feel like doing them. Out of sheer unadulterated self-will, you must simply make the choice to do them.
- When you do things, how you feel will begin to change.
- Detoxing your thinking and renewing your mind actually changes your brain chemistry. (*Who Switched Off My Brain?*,©2009 Chapter 2)
- You don't have to do them all at once. You can take basic, simple steps toward them. Celebrate the small daily steps you take toward hope
- It will be hard to do. But these things pay off for you spiritually and ultimately, emotionally.
- Sometimes you have to do things you don't feel like doing, because they will improve how you feel.

Let's go back to this idea of "taking charge" of your thinking; "taking captive" your thoughts (2 Corinthians 10:5). By our broken nature we all, mood disorder or not, suffer from "stinkin' thinkin'", or toxic thoughts. And when you and I ruminate (thinking the same thing over and over again which actually causes our brain to get stuck thinking these things), it causes even more hopelessness and despair. Here are some examples of toxic, hopeless thinking vs. the life-giving healthy thoughts one can take hold of. In other words, not allowing yourself to think the toxic, hopeless thoughts – taking them captive – and instead take hold and choose the healthy thoughts.

Toxic, Hopeless Thoughts

- I'll never get better.
- My illness/disorder can't be managed.
- God doesn't love me.
- Getting better depends only on me.
- I'm failing at this.

- My life is harder than everyone else's.
- I can't go on – I'll never make it through this.
- Death is an out for me.
- There is something wrong with me; I'm a bad person.
- No one can understand me.

Which two or three statements in this list do you allow yourself to wallow in? Copy them below; then rewrite as a positive, hope-FULL thought.

For example:
Toxic Thought: "Death is an out for me."
HopeFULL Thought: "Death is NOT an out for me."

Toxic Thought: _____

HopeFULL Thought: _____

Toxic Thought: _____

HopeFULL Thought: _____

Toxic Thought: _____

HopeFULL Thought: _____

Both hopelessness and toxic thinking lead to seeing oneself as a victim and to easily "becoming your diagnosis" – leaving you with no hope. Toxic thinking needs to be taken captive, and in choosing healthy thinking and life-giving thoughts, choosing hope will grow your faith, increase your strength to believe, and ultimately change your brain chemistry.

Oh, how I wish I had chosen sooner in my recovery to base my hope on the known God of hope, instead of wallowing in all of my feelings of hopelessness. I am an exceptional "wallower." I wallowed and I wallowed day after day following my major episode in 1995. And guess what? My hopelessness only got worse. Nearly at the point of not being able to interact with others and becoming a gigantic blob of hopelessness, one of my leaders and dear friends from the church came to visit. He sat down on the couch in our family room. I remember so little from back then, but this I remember as though it happened yesterday. Ken had his Bible with him. He opened his Bible and pulled out some half-sheets of paper and he began to read off the papers. I thought to myself, "What the heck is he doing?" He would first read a Bible passage and then he would read "points" based on the passage. What was he doing? I'll be darned, he was in fact reading notes he'd taken based upon sermons I had preached! He was preaching back the message of hope to me that I had preached to him! And while he did that, I kept thinking to myself, "Yeah, yeah, yeah, I know all of that, Ken. But you don't understand how bad I feel right now."

Ken just kept reading his notes of my sermons to me. I have no idea how long it was, but it felt like hours. But during this time something began to happen within my mind. By listening to Ken read back my own sermons, my mind began to recall those things. For those moments I began to be "airlifted" out of my hopelessness and my brain was being forced to think different thoughts than just the ruminating over and over about how hopeless I felt. I suppose you have to know Ken like I know him to understand that he was a man on a mission. When Ken was on a mission, you didn't mess with him. He didn't come to talk me through anything. He didn't come to hear me wallow. He came to preach to me the very sermons I had preached to him. And in those moments I began to choose hope. The truth began to shine like a bright light through a tiny crack in the walls of my hopelessness. It was the first tiny, tiny, TINY baby steps in choosing hope instead of hopelessness. And of all people, the Lord used Ken, one of the most disciplined people I have ever known. Ken doesn't act upon feelings unless the facts tell him to do so. And after that afternoon with Ken, I can honestly say I began to choose hope, not because I felt like it; but because it was the answer to my hopelessness. It was sure and certain because of Jesus, not because of how I felt!

Do you/have you had a "Ken" in your life? Who is/was it, and what did he/she do to motivate you to begin or continue on your road to recovery?

_____

_____

_____

_____

_____

In recovery so far, what discipline(s) are you most proud of sticking with?

_____

_____

_____

_____

_____

What disciplines tend to help you the most in dealing with hopelessness?

_____

_____

_____

_____

_____

Section 3

How Does Hope Happen?

Hope is like love. The more you give away, the more you get back. That's why there is such power in a Christian support group such as Fresh Hope. When people share their personal journeys with one another, hope is given and hope is received.

I happen to believe that hope is catching. Why? Because when I hang with people who are hopeful and full of faith, it rubs off on me. It makes me hopeful and infuses me with faith. There's a saying that says, "You become like the five people whom you spend the most time with in your life; so choose carefully who you hang around." I agree. That's why when I initially attended various support groups for those with mental health issues, I simply chose not to go back. I knew if I continued to go I would end up negative, lifeless, hopeless, and struggling to cope with my mental health issues. I wanted to live again, not simply figure out how to "cope."

Finding peers who have hope and live a life of wellness because of hope are hard to find. It would seem that the medical model for mental health has been a contributor to this idea of settling for a "less-than-full life" and learning to manage and to cope with mental health issues.

What is the difference between the medical model versus the wellness model? The medical model's focus is on the patient receiving care supervised by the help of some-one else. The focus is on someone else having the answers for what the patient needs to do in order to get better. So, the patient easily becomes very passive. They can easily find themselves believing that someone else needs to solve their problems.

It is important to note that the medical model is necessary when someone is in crisis. However the medical model for sustained recovery without the active participation of each of us in our own recovery is not helpful. Why? Because it is that exact learned helplessness that causes us to become stuck if no one is telling us what to do step by step.

In the wellness model, we take our own initiative in our recovery. We begin to see that we cannot only be active, but we can be the leader in our own recovery. After all, who's more of a specialist about us than we ourselves? We don't sit and wait for someone to tell us what to do in order to get better. Instead, we take charge of our own recovery in order to gain our lives back.

Taking back one's life after a period of sickness is, after all, what we call recovery from all health issues, not just mental health issues. For instance, if I'm in the hospital for open heart surgery, I'm certainly functioning within the medical model. Others are telling me what to do and what I'll need to do after I am released. But if I stay in that mode of others needing to tell me exactly what to do and when to do it, when I go home I would be in trouble. Returning home after a surgery like that, I need to take the initiative to see to it that I will fully recover. And the same is true with mental health issues.

Don't get me wrong; the medical model is important. And in many ways the medical model is coming to terms with its own shortcomings. But I think we all know that if you really want a transfusion of real hope, you most likely will not find it in the local psychiatric ward. When in the hospital one is usually in crisis, and merely coping at that point is key. But what about after the crisis? Following my hospital care and then adjusting to my meds, I sometimes wanted to get up on the roof of my house and scream out, "Where's the hope? I don't see any hope! Someone help… I've lost my hope!"

Knowing this, I caution you: don't buy into the idea that you need to learn to "cope" with your disorder. Don't buy into settling for a "less than what you had hoped for" life. Don't buy into the "best is behind you now" idea. Don't buy into the idea that you can't have a rich and fulfilling life. Don't buy into the idea that this is about the worst thing that could happen for you. Don't buy into other people's stigmas regarding mental health issues. And for heaven's sake, don't buy into the idea that your life isn't all that hopeful. Yes, life might be different. But different isn't hopeless, nor is it "less than" what you had hoped it to be. It's just different. Yes, you do have to come to terms with what it means to have a mental health issue. Yes, you do have to adjust some areas of your life because of it. Yes, you may have some limitations because of it. But, you do NOT have to settle with a "less than" life of hopelessness! You can *choose* hope. You can live a rich and full life in spite of your mental health issues! And becoming hope-filled happens when you:

> **You do not have to settle with a "less than" life of hopelessness!**

- Hear other people's stories of progress Being part of a positive, life-giving support group is imperative to successful recovery.
- Read and memorize Scripture.
- Give up and let God be your hope: you can finally stop striving when you realize you can't do it on your own.
- Hear how someone else "made it through" and this generates hope for you.
- Soak up God's love and mercy.
- Realize that you are not a "human doing" (worth isn't found in what we do) but rather, a "human being" who is loved by God.
- Remember that God has never left you in the past. You need to keep track of what God has done for you and to rehearse what he has done for you.
- Replace your toxic thinking and know the truth.
- You understand that real hope is not a feeling; it's a choice and a belief. It's connected to your faith, not to what you might be going through
- Understand that hope isn't like flipping a switch to "on"; it's a process.
- Understand that hope is catching.
- Understand that forgiving oneself and others brings hope.
- Understand that lies bring hopelessness.
- Understand that the Enemy wants you to feel hopeless.

Hopefully you are beginning to see that it is in fact possible to choose hope even when you feel hopeless. When you choose hope it will breathe life into you, and hope empowers you to overcome and live a full and rich life in spite of your mental health diagnosis.

It is dangerous to your recovery when you allow how you feel to determine what you do. Everyone has an occasional bad day and has bad things happen to them. But don't let those bad things define who you are. When you find yourself feeling hopeless, don't beat yourself up.

"How you think affects your emotions, feelings, relationships with others and your overall happiness in life. The way in which you think can lead you to talking yourself into, or out of, certain emotions or behaviors. Your thinking about events that occur in your life often dictates how you feel and act. It can either build a healthy or unhealthy self-esteem." [www.hellenictherapy.com]

What you think affects your feelings, and out of your feelings flow your actions. But we can change our thinking. We have hope, and we choose hope, because we know that God is on our side. Paul says in 2 Corinthians 10: 4-6:

> *"⁴ The weapons we fight with are not the weapons of the world. On the contrary, they have divine power to demolish strongholds. ⁵ We demolish arguments and every pretension that sets itself up against the knowledge of God, and we take captive every thought to make it obedient to Christ. ⁶ And we will be ready to punish every act of disobedience, once your obedience is complete."*

You are in charge of your thinking. What you think, you do. And what you do, you become. Here is a "must" verse to memorize and repeat out loud. Because of God's love, we are not consumed.

> *"Because of the LORD's great love we are not consumed, for his compassions never fail. ²³ They are new every morning; great is your faithfulness. ²⁴ I say to*

myself, 'The LORD is my portion; therefore I will wait for Him.' [25] The LORD is good to those whose hope is in Him, to the one who seeks Him; [26] it is good to wait quietly for the salvation of the LORD." Lamentations 3: 22-26

With God all things are possible. Every day His mercies are new and fresh. He loves you, and will never give up on you. He understands what's going on in you. And He wants you to enjoy the healing you have in Him. He wants your life to be good. He wants you to enjoy your life. So grab on to the fresh hope He offers to you.

Why is there such power in a Christian support group like Fresh Hope?

_____

_____

_____

_____

_____

How can reading and memorizing Scripture help bring you hope?

_____

_____

_____

_____

_____

Key Thoughts

- Choosing hope and choosing to be hopeful in spite of feeling hopeless is a key concept to recovery.
- When you are feeling totally hopeless, you must *choose* with your will through faith to remember the truth that, because of Jesus, we are never without hope.
- Thoughts and feelings of hopelessness easily take over our minds when our brain chemistry is not working properly.
- The Bible tells us that this brokenness in the world, sin, is the root cause and reason for pain, hurt, sickness, and death.
- The times you least feel like forcing yourself to do something are the times when you most need to discipline yourself to do it.
- When I take captive my negative thoughts, sooner or later my thinking will change for the positive.
- Detoxing your thinking and renewing your mind actually changes your brain chemistry.
- Support groups like Fresh Hope are powerful: When people share their personal journeys with one another, hope is given and hope is received.
- You are in charge of your thinking. You do NOT have to settle with a "less than" life of hopelessness! You can *choose* hope.
- With God, all things are possible.

Section 4

Making Tenet IV Personal

Consider what the words of Tenet IV mean to you personally. In the exercise below, rewrite Tenet IV to reflect your own life situation. Be as specific as you can.

Fresh Hope Tenet IV

My disorder can lead me to feel hopeless. Therefore, I choose to believe, regardless of my feelings, that there is help and hope for my physical, emotional, psychological and spiritual well-being.

John's Tenet IV

My mood disorder has led me to lose hope. I have allowed it to be my excuse to withdraw from interaction with my family and friends. But I realize now that I am missing out on life. I choose to believe that help and hope for me exists. Because I want to return to a place of hopefulness, I will no longer wallow in my hopelessness, but choose to seek and accept the help and support of Dr. Shaw, Fresh Hope, my family, close friends, and my accountability group. I will ask them to remind me when I am falling into toxic thinking, and I will listen to them when they encourage me with suggestions to be hope-filled.

My Tenet IV

_____

_____

_____

_____

_____

Every time you read Tenet IV, remember your purpose to be hopeful, and rejoice that you have an accountability group ready to support and love you.

Q & A with the Psychiatrist

1.   How do I know if I am really depressed or if I am choosing to be hopeless?

   Dr. Egger: If symptoms of mood change accompanied by a change in sleep, appetite, energy, or concentration, and these symptoms have persisted more than 2 weeks, this constitutes a depressive episode and not just a negative attitude.

2.   How often should I see a psychiatrist or therapist to help gauge my level of hope?

   Dr. Egger: In starting treatment, you should see your psychiatrist or therapist every one to two weeks depending on the severity of your symptoms. Medications should be reassessed every three to four weeks.

3.   I feel very hopeless today. What should I do?

   Dr. Egger: You need to seek out someone on your accountability team, a friend, pastor, or therapist. If you feel in danger of self-harm, go to the emergency room nearest you. Emergency psychiatric assistance can be arranged there.

4.   Can choosing hopeful thoughts change my brain and make it healthier?

   Dr. Egger: Choosing hopeful thoughts certainly helps sustain a healthier attitude and promotes well-being. Over time, a sustained sense of well-being may enhance brain chemistry to sustain mood.

CHAPTER 5

It's a Choice: Choose It!

TENET V

While medicine is a key component in my recovery, it is not the only answer. Therefore, I choose to explore new ways of thinking and acting in my relationships and daily living.

Together we choose freedom over suffering, and joy in living through self-knowledge in action.

"We demolish arguments and every pretension that sets itself up against the knowledge of God and we take captive every thought to make it obedient to Christ." 2 Corinthians 10:5

Section 1
Understanding the Role of Medication in Recovery

Section 2
Choosing to Be Well

Section 3
Don't Believe Everything You Feel

Section 4
Changing Your Thoughts by Trusting Your Faith

Section 5
What's Your Choice?

Section 6
Making Tenet V Personal

Wrap Up
Q & A with the Psychiatrist

Section 1

Understanding the Role of Medication in Recovery

T he vast majority of mood disorders are usually treated with some type of medicine – if not one medicine, oftentimes multiple medications. For many, finding the right medicine or the right combination of medicines can seem like a long journey of frustration after frustration. And yet, others, once diagnosed with a mood disorder, find the journey of discovering which medication works best to be relatively simple. Not everyone, of course, responds to each type of medicine exactly the same. So doctors have a challenge in finding which medicine works best for each individual. Prescribing the right medication for the right person is a delicate balance of finding the appropriate dosage, the right combination of medicines, and probably most importantly, trying to give relief to the patient as quickly as possible. While sometimes this can feel like a long, exaggerated science experiment to us, a physician friend of mine reminded me that this is why it's called the "practice" of medicine.

Medication is an important part of recovery. It requires our ability to trust our doctor and be patient to allow the medication to take effect. This can be very trying. However, it is necessary for successful recovery. It takes time, and when we don't feel well, we want the quick fix. We have to be patient in regards to our medicine working. It takes time for it to build up in our bodies and to begin regulating or correcting our brain chemistry. It takes time for the doctor to evaluate what we need and what will work for us as an individual. And then, of course, it can take time for us to feel the effects that the medicine is going to have – and sometimes the side effects.

Side effects are a big reason that many people discontinue their medication. The way the medication makes us feel at first sometimes feels worse than the actual mood disorder we've been living with. Maybe it makes us lethargic or unmotivated, maybe it contributes to weight gain, or maybe it takes away that 'up' feeling we get during our manic episodes. This is where we have to step outside our feelings, and pay attention to our thoughts and the words of those around us.

Side effects from medication are often temporary, and as we continue on the path prescribed by our doctor, our brain and body will adjust. Pushing through and looking at the long-term strategy versus how we feel today will help us stay dedicated to our treatment plan. Many medicines to treat mood disorders can take one to three months to take full effect, so it's not always best to jump off a medicine if we're just three weeks into it and experiencing some side effects. Patience is key. Although it feels like a mountain to climb some days, I encourage you to hang in there in spite of the side effects, because more times than not, the side effects will subside after a period of time. I believe there are a lot of folks who, out of impatience with the side effects, move from medicine to medicine too quickly, only to complicate and lengthen their journey to wellness.

Certainly, medicines have greatly improved in the last 25 years, and the numbers and types of medicines for the treatment of mood disorders have grown exponentially. We can be encouraged by what will be available in the future. With awareness, research, and time, many new medications and ways to treat these disorders will be developed.

Have you visited with a doctor (psychiatrist) to evaluate your mood disorder and determine if medication is needed? Have you been patient long enough to let your medicine(s) work?

_____

_____

_____

_____

How do you feel about taking medicine to feel better?

_____

_____

_____

_____

_____

How do you feel about the potential of the medicine having side effects, and what is your greatest fear? Are you willing to "wait out" the side effects so that you might receive the benefits of a particular medicine that your doctor believes will work for you?

_____

_____

_____

_____

_____

Are you compliant with taking your medicines daily as prescribed? If not, why not? If you don't take your medicine as prescribed, have you told your doctor that you are not compliant with taking your medicine?

_____

_____

_____

_____

_____

How can a relationship with the Lord help you stay the course as you work with your doctor to determine an appropriate treatment plan? How can the Lord help calm your fears?

_____

_____

_____

_____

_____

Section 2

Choosing to Be Well

Hopefully we have gained some insight into the importance of medication in our recovery plan. However, the bottom line in this tenet and the bottom line for us to grasp and understand in our own recovery is the fact that medicine doesn't do it all. Medicine is a key part, but it's not the only thing that will help us regain our hope for living a full and rich life. I like to think of it this way. Recovery runs on two parallel tracks: the first track is the medical track - working with our doctor to evaluate our situation, the doctor prescribing the medication, and the medicine working on our brain chemistry. The second track, the other part of a successful recovery, is our thought track - the decisions and choices that we make in both our actions and how we think.

Medicine is the first component of successful recovery, because it helps our brain chemistry to stabilize. We must accept this as part of our wellness plan. But if that's all we do, take a pill every day and hope everything will get better, our recovery will most likely be limited and short-lived. The other half of successful recovery, just as significant in many respects, is making the right choices, controlling our thinking, and taking our thoughts captive.

As our medicine begins to work, then we can work in regards to our thinking and our actions. We can come alongside the medicine as it changes our brain chemistry and we can begin to change how we think. We can also begin to change how we act and react in situations. We can't just take our medicine and sit back and wait for it to work, somehow believing that it's going to change how we think and act. If that were the case, diet pills would have worked a long, long time ago. Comparatively, if we were trying to lose weight and we began to take diet pills, but decided to go ahead and eat cupcakes for breakfast, lunch, and dinner, we most likely wouldn't lose weight. With those of us with a mood disorder, taking a pill but continuing to think negative thoughts or choosing to believe lies about ourselves won't allow us to get better or live a hope-filled life. It simply does not work that way. Instead, while the medicine works on its track to regulate our brain chemistry, you and I have to work on our track to straighten out our thinking and our behaviors.

That's what we mean in Tenet V when we say, "while medicine is a key component in my recovery, medicine alone does not solve everything." Therefore we have to choose to gain insight into thinking differently and doing things differently. In other words, we've got to think differently and we've got to act differently in our relationships and in our daily living.

The medical model that we have learned as patients, in some respects teaches us a learned helplessness. Our brains aren't working right, so we feel we need to hand over our entire life to someone else to handle. Right? We begin to believe that somehow, somebody else, usually with the letters MD behind his/her name, is going to 'fix' what's wrong with us by giving us a pill. Or a counselor is going to listen to our story and talk us through our troubles and make it all better. Somebody else is going to help us deal with our relationships, our financial situation, and our future. Somebody else is going to have the answers. In fact, sometimes we can feel so much that way that we don't even trust ourselves.

The reality is that we are our own most significant advocates. We're the people who can make our recovery a reality. We can choose to get better. Fresh Hope empowers you and me to be in charge of our own recovery; it's self-empowerment!

You and I have an active role in our recovery because changing our thinking and our behaviors means that we have to DO something. We have to take an active part. The part that we have to take is to make a decision: "Will I or won't I change? Will I or won't I change how I think, how I react, how I look at my situation?" It's a decision of our will. It's a decision of our mind, not our brain. It's a decision of willpower that needs to be made no matter how miserable we feel, how incompetent we feel, or how hopeless we feel. This decision is an everyday decision. Sometimes we don't even realize it when we make it. We just simply need to keep saying it to ourselves each day: "I choose. I choose to change my thinking. I choose to change my actions." And sooner or later, we begin to change.

Put very simply: Choose it! You can't heal what you refuse to confront.

Do you feel your recovery tracks (medical and thought) are running parallel? If one is running off course right now, which one, and what can you do to get back "on track"?

_____

_____

_____

_____

_____

How have you seen your reactions and feelings change with the help of your medication?

_____

_____

_____

_____

_____

How has your participation in Fresh Hope (or another support group) empow-ered you in your choices and recovery?

_____

_____

_____

_____

_____

Section 3

Don't Believe Everything You Feel

Before you continue reading, take a few moments and answer the following questions.

What feelings do you experience most of the time throughout the day (i.e. happy, sad, angry, excited, nervous, etc.)?

_____

_____

_____

_____

_____

Would you describe yourself as a positive or a negative person? Why?

_____

_____

_____

_____

_____

_____

Do you believe that your feelings oftentimes determine your actions? How, and when?

_____

_____

_____

_____

_____

What role do you believe that God plays in your recovery?

_____

_____

_____

_____

_____

When I was first diagnosed with having bipolar disorder, I was so glad that they had a name for what I felt and experienced. I was so glad that this "mood monster" that was within me was not <u>me</u>, but it was something else. I wanted to find out everything I could, not only about the mood monster, but also how that mood monster had affected me.

I was excited to change. I really was. I wanted to find out what I needed to change in my thinking, how I needed to understand things, and look at life differently. I wanted to change my behaviors so that I could feel better, so that I could have better relationships. By that point I had experienced so much pain in my life, I didn't want any more. So I was ready to listen, and I was willing to act. The pain of being "sick" was so much greater than the pain of changing; I was willing to do whatever was necessary.

As I've observed people over the years, I've come to the conclusion that there are really only two kinds of people when it comes to making decisions. One kind says, "I'm going to decide to do this." And they just do it. For these folks, the only factor is their will. Maybe we've met some of these people. When they choose to lose weight, they just lose it. Or they decide to run a marathon, or write a book, and they are able to direct their whole lives towards accomplishing that goal and seeing it through to completion.

Then there are those of us who seemingly only learn to change or do something differently when we have no other alternative but to change; when things get difficult enough and we are nearly forced into a new way. We only change when there's been enough pain.

Since you're reading and working through these tenets, I suspect you have had significant pain in your life and have reached your limit to cause you to want to change. Pain, typically, is a great motivator.

If this describes you and you've experienced enough pain and hurt that you are ready to change, your next question probably is, "How"?

First, we must make the decision right now that we are going to do whatever it takes to get better; that we are going to gain insights into thinking differently, look at things differently—and interact with and react to people differently. Once that decision is made, we then can begin to have others help and support us. We can find and draw strength and insights from others – from our therapists, from our doctors, from our pastors, and from our friends and loved ones. We can also find great support in peer support groups, such as Fresh Hope. We can also gain a lot of knowledge and insight by reading books, conducting our own research, and educating ourselves on our disorder.

As we learn and listen, we begin to understand that the effects of the imbalance of our brain chemistry have caused a lot of behaviors that do not help us in our recovery. And many times, these thoughts actually sidetrack and inhibit our recovery. The chemical imbalance in our brains has resulted in a lot of negative and toxic thinking.

As we begin the recovery process, let's identify some of the behaviors that we have developed that are not helpful.

For instance, if we've been suffering from severe depression, we might have spent a lot of time in bed, a lot of time with the shades pulled, in a dark room, sleeping all day, up all night. We have been held captive by our feelings, and our thoughts have kept us isolated and swimming in a pool of negative self-talk. None of this behavior or way of thinking is helpful to us in recovery.

We may not be keeping a regimented schedule, because we don't feel like it. We don't go to bed at a decent hour because we don't feel tired, or we don't get up, shower, and get dressed in the morning because it just feels like too much work. By not doing these things, we hinder our recovery process.

In our struggles with anxiety, we might have developed the problem of being on time, or following through on scheduled activities with friends. The medicine may start to take the edge off the anxiety, but if we don't get on the right track and decide with our mind and our will that we're going to be on time, that we're going to follow through, that we're going to do what we said we were going to do, recovery will be stalled or stopped.

One of the most important things that I've learned to understand in my own recovery is that I don't always need to yield to what I feel. In other words, there can be times when I feel anxious, or my mood has dipped and I don't feel great about the day. But I don't have to yield to those feelings. It's a choice to allow these feelings to dictate my thoughts and then my actions. I can, with my mind and with my will, push through it – and so can you.

Maybe we have scheduled a social engagement with friends and just don't feel like going. We've had a stressful week, we're feeling anxious about leaving the house, and really want to give an excuse to get out of the plans for the evening. Our feelings are telling us to just stay home, blame it on our brain, and crawl into bed. But it's important to push through and to go, especially early on in our recovery.

There are going to be many things we need to do and have to do, but don't feel like doing. We've gotten very used to yielding to how we feel, and to giving in to the feelings that keep us from participating in healthy activities that are part of living life. Very quickly in the recovery process I learned that many times I simply needed to do something even though I desperately did not feel like it – and my feelings would catch up.

Right after my major episode in the spring of 1995, I not only was severely clinically depressed, but I also became agoraphobic. Leaving the house would simply send me into a panic attack. Donna, my wife, was well aware of this. So periodically she would say to me, "We are going for ice cream this afternoon. You have to go no matter what. The only choice you have in the matter is which Dairy Queen we are going to. Period." She would have to nearly pull me out of the house. I would beg and plead with her to simply leave me at home. I would have done anything to get out of going. But, she knew better than to let me off the hook. Inevitably I would end up coming home feeling better. I began to learn that in order to overcome, I sometimes was going to have to do things that every fiber of my being did NOT want to do.

In recovery, you and I must pay attention to how we feel, but not always act based on those feelings. Or at least not act the way we always have in the past when our moods were the boss.

Feelings versus Moods

Knowing the difference between a feeling and a mood is extremely important for experiencing success in recovery. Why? If you do not understand the difference between the two, you can easily mistake a feeling as your mood - which can become very confusing in knowing what your actual mood is at the time. As one who is being treated for a mood disorder, you need to closely monitor any mood changes. We also need to learn how to process our feelings. But, if you mistakenly confuse a feeling for a mood, your "mood" can easily seem as though it is something that it is not.

For example, let's say that my mood is a 3.5 on a 1 to 5 scale, with 1 being an extremely dark mood with suicidal ideations (thoughts) and 5 being close to mania. And as I'm experiencing this mood of 3.5, I end up having a conflict with a close friend and begin to feel hurt, fearful, and frustrated. At this point I'm simply feeling hurt and frustrated by my friend's actions, and fearful that the friendship might end. These are feelings due to a circumstance. These feelings do not necessarily change or threaten the stability of my mood. As long as I work through my feelings in a healthy and appropriate way, my feelings will pass with time. It's normal to experience feelings due to different things that happen in daily life.

According to Laura Giles, LCSW, feelings (emotions) are influenced by the environment and are usually directed towards a specific object. Feelings also tend to come and go quickly. For example, I may get angry at another driver when I am cut off in traffic. When I am angry, my blood pressure rises, my face turns red, my voice gets tighter, and I become less flexible, more excitable, and less rational. When we realize we are experiencing an emotion, we can usually tell what triggered it and can often do something to change it.

A mood is also a feeling state, but it lasts longer and may not have an obvious trigger. For example, when you wake up in the morning feeling cranky, and it lasts all day, that would be a mood. When you are in a mood state, you tend to look for opportunities to justify the mood. So when you are cranky, you see traffic, your boss, and being late as reasons to sustain the mood.

Dr. Tim Hill, psychologist, explains the 'layering' of emotions and moods in this way: We experience emotions at the same time as moods, but emotions seem to 'sit on top' of moods. For instance, when you're in a bad mood it is quite possible to have brief feelings of happiness and joy. Similarly, when in a good mood, it is still possible to have sad or angry feelings. However, it is much more likely that your mood will influence how you feel so that the two appear the same. In this way, our emotions are susceptible to the mood we are in, and this also makes us more likely to interpret our environment in particular ways and distort our thinking. When we are in a bad mood, it is much easier to misinterpret things in the light of this bad mood.

We can also understand the difference between feelings and moods by using the weather model [from www.depressionmentalhealth.com.] Your mood is like the climate of a region (i.e., temperate, arid, tropical, arctic). But an individual feeling is like the weather trends of a climate, (i.e., rain in the tropics, blizzards in the arctic). The weather is temporary, just as feelings change. Mood is more of an ever-present or sustained emotion – your personal 'climate'. Feelings are the calms and storms of weather within your life.

It is important to distinguish between the two because many people are hesitant to feel their feelings: they fear becoming overwhelmed, getting out of control, or having things escalate into undesirable behavior. If you understand that emotions are short lived, it may make it easier to 'sit' with them, feel them, and watch them change into something else. Getting clear on these differences will help you better understand yourself and others.

Another reason to distinguish between feelings and moods is that how you cope through them is different. If you are in an emotion (feeling) state, relax, experience it, and then watch it go. If you are in a mood state, you may have to take active steps to cope because it will last a while.

Moods and feelings are similar, but not the same. Understanding the differences can help you deal with them effectively and lose your fear of them.

Later in the book, we will talk about the importance of self-care and identifying those instances when we do need to take time for ourselves in order to prevent our brain from entering an extreme high or low spot. However, as we are working through this Tenet, keep in mind that most of the time, to think and act differently, we have to curb our feelings and not allow them to rule our lives. This is the only way to truly feel better in the long run.

Recently, I've been around someone who experienced a relapse in her depression. I can see that her depressed mood is making her feel like she doesn't have a choice about getting better. But I keep encouraging her. I say, "I hope to see you at group this week" and "I hope you will visit with your doctor about your medication," or "I hope to hear from you and we can talk." But sadly, all of my encouragements and offerings of support have fallen on deaf ears, because at this point she's not able to see that her feelings and mood are controlling her life. For this individual, once she is able to step away from her feelings (which will most likely occur when her medication has been adjusted), then she will know that the things I am suggesting are actually good for her recovery.

Knowing it and doing it are two different things. Most people, if they want to lose weight, know that eating healthy and exercising is the way to take off extra pounds. If we know those things but don't do them, the weight isn't going anywhere, except maybe up. The same is true in mental health recovery. We can know it, but if we don't do it, we won't get better.

We must make the choice to detox our thoughts and renew our minds.

There's a book written by Julie Fast, a blogger, in regards to mental health issues.

It's entitled, "Get It Done When We're Depressed: 50 Strategies for Keeping Our Life on Track." That's the reality. You and I can still choose and exercise our will, especially once the medication is right and starts to kick in.

We *can* change how we act, our behavior patterns, how we do things, and our routines – even when we don't feel like it. And we can change how we look at things. Instead of looking through black glasses, we can look at the world through clear glasses and be realistic and positive.

I know it may come as a surprise to some that we really do have the power to choose. Depending where you are at in recovery, it may seem nearly absurd

Think differently – fight back!

to you. This ability to choose may be very diminished if you're extremely depressed, extremely sick, extremely manic, or extremely anxious. It may be so diminished that even the choices you are able to make

in the right direction may seem very meaningless. But I would encourage you with whatever ability you have, even if ever so slight, ever so little – use it! Use it to make a choice to think differently and fight back!

I don't know about you, but for me, just knowing that I have the ability to make some choices in my recovery is extremely empowering, even if those choices may not feel significant at the time. It is very encouraging to know that I can choose different actions, and I can choose different thinking. What encouraging news it is to know that it's not just the medicine 'fixing' me. It's me, making choices for myself each day to turn my negative thoughts into positive ones, which in turn will help me feel better.

Earlier in this chapter I discussed two types of decision-makers, one proactive and determined, the other reactive and reluctant. Well, some of us might actually be stuck somewhere in the middle.

For those of us who easily make decisions and we simply choose to do what we need to do: Good for you! Make it! Choose it!

For those of us who learn only by pain, we've only prolonged it. But if you've experienced a lot of pain, maybe you're just purely ready, like I was, to make the decisions to change.

But maybe you're not sure. Maybe you've experienced a great deal of pain but you still have doubts about whether or not you will be able to really change your thinking and behaviors. You might be thinking, "Do I really need to do this? Is there really a problem?" In this case, I encourage you to trust and listen to those around you. Pay attention and take notes of the things in this book that apply to you. Hear out the loved ones around you and their opinions about your moods and behaviors. Seek the opinion of a doctor you trust. You can either trust what everyone around you is saying, or you can choose not to believe their words. If you choose not to, it is likely that until the pain of your situation is greater than the pain of recovery, you will stay exactly where you are now.

After reading this section, do you see any pattern in your usual thoughts that needs to change?

What is the difference between a feeling and a mood?

_____

_____

_____

_____

How is your life being dictated by your thoughts and feelings?

_____

_____

_____

_____

What specific behaviors or actions have been influenced by the way you typically <u>feel</u>?

_____

_____

_____

_____

Name two things that you can choose to look at differently in your recovery.

1. _____

_____

_____

_____

2. _____

_____

_____

_____

From whom or what do you most draw your strength and insight? Write out a memorable instance that continues to be a motivator in your recovery.

_____

_____

_____

_____

Section 4

Changing Your Thoughts by Trusting Your Faith

Changing the way we think is not only about recognizing when we are in the middle of toxic thoughts, but also accepting God's role in our lives and in our recovery.

Paul tells us in the New Testament that we're supposed to take captive every thought. And in taking captive every thought, he also tells us that we're supposed to think on the good things. We're supposed to think on that which is good, and right, and pure, and all these great things. Yet, so often, our thinking is negative. It's toxic. It literally is bad, negative self-talk. And if we don't change that negative self-talk, then our thinking will continue to pollute our minds, even while the medicine is trying to get our brain chemistry straightened out.

Have you ever said or thought any – or a version of – these phrases about yourself?

- "Nobody understands what I'm going through."
- "Things have never been worse."
- "My situation will never get any better."
- "This is the best it will ever be."
- "Everyone is against me."
- "I'm broken, ruined, devastated, etc."
- "I'm being punished."
- "My life is awful."
- "I won't ever have the life I wanted."
- "I won't ever get back the life I had."

If we were sitting together and you said any of the above phrases, I would of course remind you that none of these things are true. They are all toxic, self-destructive thoughts based on lies we believe about ourselves and our situation. Our feelings take over and guide our thoughts into stinkin' thinkin'. Stinkin' thinkin' will destroy our days, our lives, our relationships, our jobs, and anything else it can get its arms wrapped around. It will lead us to believe that we are worthless, that life is hopeless, and that the world is against us. Remember, the Bible tells us that Satan is the father of all lies. Satan lies, kills, and destroys.

The key questions are: How do we combat this negative self-talk? How do we rid ourselves of stinkin' thinkin'? Through faith in God; by His truth setting us free.

One of the things that so easily happen when we don't take charge of our thinking and of our thoughts is that we begin to ruminate. Ruminating is one of those things that happens when you start to think about one thought – a negative thought or a worry – and you begin to think it over and over and over again. Interestingly enough, when the brain is left to 'think about whatever it wants to think about,' it actually digs in negative thoughts and worries like a groove in the old vinyl records. The needles would often get stuck in the record grooves, and replay the same music over and over until the needle was moved out of that groove. When our brains begin to think over and over and over something that is negative (negative self-talk, for instance), this creates a "groove," an electrical thought pattern that doesn't stop. And then we're stuck emotionally and seemingly can't get past it. So what do we do about it? We have to take charge of our thoughts and what we allow ourselves to think about. But how?

Well, here's how I was able to overcome what had been a lifetime of ruminating until I began the recovery process:

- First, I identified my negative self-talk. For instance, I would say things to myself like, "You're not going to be able to do this and you might as well already give up right now," and "You are a failure." I actually sat down and made the list out. It took a while to compile the list. Even once I thought I was done with it, I would still run across things.

  The easiest way to start identify the ruminating thoughts is simply listen to your "inner-thinking." What is it that worries you? What are the things that you think over and over? Simply write them down. Those are the thought patterns that have routed out a groove in your brain.

- After I created my list, I then identified what was so "stinkin'" about each thought. In other words, what in my "stinkin' thinkin'" either wasn't true or needed to be looked at positively and from a faith perspective? I wrote those things down opposite the ruminating thoughts.

- Then came the most interesting and unique thing that I did which worked for me to overcome. Every time I began to have "stinkin' thinkin'" or began to ruminate and worry about something, I would begin to talk out loud to myself. The first thing I would say was, "Stop it, Brad." If what I was saying was not true, then I would say, "You know this is not true!" And then I would say what was true. By my brain actually hearing my voice, it interrupted the negative pattern it kept replaying.

- After that, I would simply tell myself (out loud) to stop thinking that! And I would quote Paul's words to "think on those things" which are good, right, pure, etc. (Philippians 4:8). There were times when I could not say these things out loud. For example, if I was with other people or in a public place, I would simply say it to myself in my thoughts. But it always worked best by actually saying these things out loud to myself. I was told that this is because the brain becomes a bit "startled" into listening to your voice, and as a result would immediately begin to stop repeating the ruminating thought.

And if I failed to stop thinking it and began to think it again, I would not allow myself to use that as an excuse for not fighting it. Too often we simply get lazy in recovery (cause it is hard work and can become exhausting) and we give up using the excuse, "I just can't do it. It doesn't work for me."

- Then the hardest part would be that I would NOT allow myself to think that thought again. And I would change what I was thinking about or doing. Sometimes I actually had to start focusing on a project or something else. But

I did not dare let my brain repeat that same thought. This was very hard to do. But, I would tell myself, "Stop obsessing about this – you are just causing the "groove of ruminating" to get deeper on something that is either not true or not helpful, or both.

- And believe it or not, after many months of this, I was able to overcome a lot of the "stinkin' thinkin'" and in a very tangible way I experienced what I have come to call "pushing through."

I'm certainly no doctor. And there are probably many folks who could give you a scientific, physiological explanation as to why this worked for me. I offer it to you in my simple, practical way that worked for me as a possibility of working for you, too.

This is important work to do! Too often we just let our brains determine what we are going to think about. And instead, you tell your brain what you will and won't think about. You take charge of it. After all, most of us say we believe that the Bible is completely true. So, why would Paul tell you to take your thoughts captive if that were not possible to do? Yes, I know, on this side of heaven nothing is perfect. But that does not mean that we cannot do either some or most of these sorts of things. Too often we use excuses like this to avoid the hard work that is before us. Aren't we new creations in Christ? Aren't we empowered by the Holy Spirit? Yes, of course we are! This is why, for me, creating a support group that drew upon Christ and the power He gives us was so important. Because without Him and the power of His Holy Spirit – the best you have is you! And I don't know about you, but I do know about me – and I'm not all that strong in and of myself. But, I CAN do all things through Christ Who not only strengthens me – but, empowers me to even take captive my thinking.

Now, if you are not able to experience some success and achievements with your ruminating, then you might want to talk with your doctor. There are medicines that can help you. But I caution you to not look for medicine to do any of the "hard work" that you first should try to do on your own. It's too easy to want to "numb" out on medicine and not really do the hard work of recovering and taking back your life.

As Christians we need to always remember Who our God is and what He has done for us through Christ. The truth is: God isn't going to let us down. He will not forsake us and He will continue to be with us, no matter how we feel or how much stinkin' thinkin' we might have.

So instead, in recovery, we need to think positively. We need to think from a faith perspective as Christians. Choosing to believe will allow us to see the truth. The truth is that all things are possible through Jesus and that no matter how we feel, what disorder we have been diagnosed with and how bad things seem, through our faith in the Lord, we can overcome and will be loved for eternity.

Just imagine the power of taking just 10 minutes a day to thank the Lord. Just imagine starting every single day with 10 minutes of ONLY thanking the Lord and being filled with gratitude – no matter what your situation might be. The power of a grateful spirit will begin to change how you see everything – including any difficult circumstances.

God will help us with our choices.

In her book, *Who Switched Off My Brain?*, Dr. Caroline Leaf identifies how our thoughts change our brains and bodies – for better or for worse. "Even though you can't always control your circumstances, you can make fundamental choices that will help you control your reaction to your circumstances and keep toxic input out of your brain." (*Who Switched Off My Brain?*, 2009, p.54). I encourage you to check out her website at www.drleaf.com. Here she identifies ways for us to detox our brains to start thinking differently and renew our minds. While she and I differ in how we regard medication and mental health issues, I wholeheartedly agree with her about changing our thinking. And certainly she knows far more about the scientific workings of the brain than I. Like Paul says in Romans 12:2, "Be transformed by the renewing of our minds" through God's Word. You have far more ability to choose what you think than what you "think" you do!

Read the following Scripture passages and reflect on their meaning. Write down some notes as they relate to your recovery.

Romans 5:1-5

_____

_____

_____

_____

_____

Psalm 119:105

_____

_____

_____

_____

_____

Many times, we must actually tell ourselves out loud to stop thinking a certain thought that is ruminating in our brain. Write a phrase that you can say out loud to God each time you need to change a thought pattern. For example, when I'm thinking, "I can never be forgiven for this," I will say, "Here's the truth: If I confess my sins, God promises I <u>am</u> forgiven." (1 John 1:9)

_____

_____

_____

_____

_____

Section 5

What's Your Choice?

As we wrap up this chapter, I want to take some time and ask, "What do you want to choose? Do you want to choose to change how you look at things, how you think, how you act, and especially, how you interact in relationships? Do you want to choose to become your true self as opposed to the real you being clouded by a disorder?

To get rid of that stinkin' thinkin' and the associated behaviors means that we are going to have to trust feedback from other people – safe people of course; people that we trust (your circle of accountability described in Chapter 3). We're going to have to ask them for feedback. We're going to have to give them permission to give us feedback. We're going to need to work with our therapists. We're going to need to be talking with other peers, hopefully in a support group of some sort. If not in Fresh Hope, there are many other mental health support groups out there that can be extremely helpful. All of this is to help us understand how we're seeing things and reacting to things, so that we can identify those moments when our feelings are dictating our lives. That's when it's time to stop, and choose to think differently.

We will need to exercise our faith. This will mean choosing to believe that God is Who He says He is, even though we may feel doubtful; that God hasn't left us, even though we may feel abandoned and alone; that God still loves us, even though we may feel worthless and incapable of giving or receiving love.

I once joined a health club. The exercise equipment was on the second floor, up a long flight of stairs. The steam room, sauna, pool, lounge, and snack bar were on the first floor. Everything I needed was on the 1st floor, and I never went up those steps. After many visits to the steam room but not to the exercise room, a trainer took notice, and challenged me to climb those steps. I took that challenge – eventually – and thought I had succeeded – until the trainer indicated that was only the first step. Now that I was up there, he expected me to actually use the machines!

We as a church are like this – many of us believe we're being good Christians by going to church on Sunday. But that exposure does little good without personal investment. We need to exercise our faith, not just hear the sermon. People know the Bible, but don't put it into action. And contrary to what many believe, head knowledge does not equal faith. So you and I must choose to follow the words of Paul, and "take captive every thought" (2 Corinthians 10.5). I'm going "to the second floor." How about you?

He loves us unconditionally, and through our faith we choose to believe in Him despite of our feelings.

Choosing to overcome and not play the victim.

Choosing to say, "I can overcome this. Life can be good again. Why? Because my God is able."

Choosing to tell our disorder, "Sit down and shut up."

And very simply, choose not to ever, ever give up.

These things are self-knowledge. How we act and how we think, having a knowledge of ourselves, and changing how we do things, will bring freedom from suffering over pain – and suddenly joy will take its place.

One of my greatest joys in the last three years has been that I have seen the pain that I've gone through help others, because that pain has given me insight. It's helped me to change. That pain has enabled me to think differently. That self-knowledge and the actions that I've taken based upon that self-knowledge has brought about significant change in my life. And just watching, talking with me, or hearing my story has helped and encouraged untold amounts of people in knowing that they, too, can have the same thing. They can have freedom from suffering over pain, and that joy in living is possible, in spite of having a mood disorder.

In fact, that's the real bottom line, and we'll end where we began: It's a choice. Choose it.

What do you choose?

_____

_____

_____

_____

_____

_____

What actions will you take to get rid of your stinkin' thinkin'?

_____

_____

_____

_____

_____

Key Thoughts

- Medicine is a key part, but it's not the only thing that will help us regain our hope for living a full and rich life.
- Pushing through any side effects and looking at the long-term strategy versus how we feel today will help us stay dedicated to our treatment plan.
- Medicine is just the first component of getting better; the majority of a successful recovery is making the right choices, controlling our thinking, and taking our thoughts captive.
- Do not allow your feelings to dictate your thoughts and actions.
- Ruminating can get you stuck in your recovery.
- We must make the choice: to detox our thoughts and renew our minds.
- In recovery, we must pay attention to how we feel, but not always act based on those feelings.
- Moods and feelings (emotions) are different. Feelings are triggered by events; moods last longer and often do not have triggers.
- God isn't going to let us down. He will not forsake us and He will continue to be with us, no matter how we feel or how much stinkin' thinkin' we might have.
- Joy in living is possible, in spite of having a mood disorder. It's a choice. Choose it.

Section 6

Making Tenet V Personal

Consider what the words of Tenet V mean to you personally. In the exercise below, rewrite Tenet V to reflect your own life situation. Be as specific as you can.

Fresh Hope Tenet V

While medicine is a key component in my recovery, it is not the only answer. Therefore, I choose to explore new ways of thinking and acting in my relationships and daily living.

John's Tenet V

My medications are necessary to my recovery, but they don't do it all. I have to be proactive and dedicated to my recovery. Therefore, I choose to establish and follow a daily schedule, and I choose to take action to get rid of my stinkin' thinkin'.

My Tenet V

_____

_____

_____

_____

_____

Every time you read Tenet V, honor your promise to be proactive in your recovery to improve your thinking and quality of recovery.

Q & A with the Psychiatrist

1. How do I know what medication is right for me?

    Dr. Egger: Selecting a medication is not trial and error. Medications are prescribed based upon groups of symptoms rather than just an official diagnosis. Try to describe for your physician exactly what symptoms you have: i.e. anxiety, depression, rapid or slowed thinking, thoughts of self-harm, insomnia, or appetite disturbance, in as much detail as you can. Later compare if your symptoms improve, stay the same, or worsen after starting medication.

2. How long will it take for me to find a medication that works?

    Dr. Egger: Each medication tier tried will take 2-3 months to adjust and determine if it is helping.

3. Will I have to be on medication for the rest of my life?

    Dr. Egger: If symptoms have occurred more than two times, i.e. mania, depression, or thought disturbance, then yes.

4. I just can't seem to get my life together, how do I know if I'm making the right choices?

    Dr. Egger: You need to seek out an accountability partner to help determine if decisions and choices are appropriate or not.

5.   I have always been this way. How will I ever get my brain to change and think differently?

Dr. Egger: You cannot change your brain but you can change your attitude toward your illness and living with it. Medications may induce positive changes in brain function over time.

CHAPTER 6

Living a Rich Life: In Spite of It

TENET VI

At times I have allowed myself to become a victim, "defined" by my disorder. Therefore I choose to overcome and live in hope and joy, in spite of my disorder.

Together, we share in each other's victories and celebrate the whole person.

"For God has not given us a spirit of fear, but of power and love and a sound mind." 2 Timothy 1:7

Section 1
Victim vs. Victor

Section 2
Surviving or Thriving?

Section 3
The Role of Christ in Recovery

Section 4
Finding Hope

Section 5
God's Purpose for Pain

Section 6
Making Tenet VI Personal

Wrap Up
Q & A with the Psychiatrist

Section 1

Victim vs. Victor

O ne of the most inspiring people I've had in my life for the last 10 years, in regards to my own recovery and just approaching life in general, has been my nephew, Tait.

When Tait was 14 years old, he was in a terrible school bus accident. It was a beautiful October afternoon, and I got a call that there had been a bus accident and my nephews were both being life-flighted to the hospital. My sister, their mother, was there. She was in the bus behind them. Her only two kids were on the bus in front of her that fell off a bridge construction area, doing a ¾ roll in the air and landing in a ravine.

Tait was the first one airlifted from the scene. He had an injured leg, a cracked pelvis, a collapsed lung, and a compound fracture in his arm. But even more severe was the serious trauma he suffered to his brain.

I'll never forget that day. I've never experienced anything like that in my life before. I hope to not have to go through anything like it ever again. I watched my sister collapse, just folding up like an accordion, when she walked into the room and saw her son unconscious and on life-support. I remember my dad pleading with God to take him and leave Tait; so Tait could have a full life. It was difficult for everyone.

It was a big interruption to their lives. Of course, it was a huge interruption for Tait and to the lives of his parents and brother.

They told us that Tait probably wouldn't make it past the first 12 hours. When 12 hours had passed, the doctor came in and said, "Well, now we're going to have to wait and see, until he's stable."

They told my sister that one of the things that could help his brain in recovery would be to keep him thinking about the normal routines of daily living. And so she would take a little toothpaste smeared onto a cotton ball and hold it under his nose while she talked about him brushing his teeth. They would put his tennis shoes on and she would say to him, "Now it's time to go to school," or as she took his shoes off later in the day, "Now you're getting home from school."

They played old videos of Nebraska football games on the TV in his room. He was a very good football player, even as a freshman in high school. The next week he was going to get to start suiting up and working out with the varsity team. He had dreams and hopes of playing for the University of Nebraska.

He was an energetic kid, had a positive attitude, and enjoyed taking in all of life. And now to see him laying still, in a coma on life support, was so very difficult.

When Tait lived past a few days and they said he was stable – after having had surgery on his arm – I remember the doctors saying that his brain would most likely never recover. One of the nurses took me aside and said, "You might want to help your family prepare for Tait living non-responsive for the rest of his life." That was so painful to hear.

Somehow, sometime in those first few weeks, Tait opened his eyes. And when he did, it was remarkable! The nurses were surprised. The doctors were surprised. Still, they again prepared us that this might be as good as it gets.

But then, he started following us in the room with his eyes. The doctors kept warning us that in any phase of his recovery, Tait could get stuck, or that he could even revert to an earlier stage. And then of all surprises, after a little while longer, Tait began to talk! It was so thrilling. The hospital staff said they had never seen anything quite like this kind of recovery. As far as we were concerned, it was a miracle.

Once Tait began to speak, and his vitals were stable, they transferred him to a different hospital that specifically helps people with brain injuries. After the move, however, he quit talking and instead began making these strange noises, kind of like the noise you would expect an animal in heat to make.

It was difficult to be around him. I felt so sorry for my sister and her husband, because day after day after day, they were there in his room. They took turns 24/7 to be with him; helping him and encouraging him. Whatever they told my sister and her husband to do that would help him in his recovery, they would do it. They would follow it to the letter.

One night, I offered to stay with Tait so my sister and brother-in-law might take a break. He was making so many noises, I just couldn't sleep. Even with earplugs, the sound was deafening. At about 4 o'clock in the morning, I finally gave up on trying to sleep. The only time he didn't make the noise was if he was chewing. So I fed him little cookies until about 8:00 am, when it was time for breakfast. He would just gnaw on those cookies, or gnaw on some ice, and while gnawing he wasn't making noise.

Through the recovery process, he started talking again. Even after this amazing accomplishment and all his progress, his doctors and nurses told his family that he probably wouldn't laugh or cry or experience many emotions. They said that many times when there's been a brain injury, emotions seem to fade and many times the effect is flat.

But not my nephew! Nope. Not Tait. I walked into the room to visit him after he began talking again, and he said,

"Hi, Uncle Brad!"

And I said, "You're talking!"

And he said, "Yup!"

I said, "So, do you remember when I spent the night with you?"

He said, "Oh, yeah."

"I slept right there in that bed, but I had my back to you because of those noises you were making. I had my back to you the whole night."

And he said, "Yeah, I remember."

I said, "Well, what do you remember?"

And he said, "I remember your big butt. Your big, enormous butt!"

And then he laughed and the rest of us cried tears of joy.

We cried tears of joy because Tait was recovering and healing. His recovery was so remarkable that even today it seems so surreal, because here was somebody who wasn't supposed to make it. He was supposed to be a vegetable, non-functioning. But he's not. He's alive and living. No, it's not the life he or his parents thought he would be living. But, in spite of his circumstances his life is full and rich. He is choosing to live.

Tait is still overcoming a lot. Today, he's in a wheelchair most of the time. He can walk with some help. He also has some short-term memory issues. There are other issues, I'm sure, that he's had, that I'm not even aware of. But I marvel at how Tait and his Mom and Dad and brother have handled the situation. It's an amazing story of perseverance, overcoming odds, and never giving up.

And through it all, I've never heard Tait complain about what happened. He was the victim of a horrific school bus crash, yet I've never heard him complain. I've never heard him rant or rave about it or say, "Why me?" He just accepts that things are what they are, and he's going to make the best of it. Amazing.

There have been moments when he's grieved. My sister and her husband and Tait's brother have grieved. We as his family have grieved, too. But there came a point where it was time to get on with life.

Tait graduated from high school, with some help, of course. On graduation day, he was accompanied to the stage by his paraprofessional aid, and as he received his diploma, people cheered uncontrollably. With a smile, Tait just couldn't help himself and took a big bow.

Tait has been an inspiration to me, an incredible example of getting on with life. He's helped me to see how it's possible to have joy and hope, and live a rich and full life in spite of something.

My nephew has gone on to take some college courses. He attends a couple of Nebraska football games every year. They've even gone to some Bowl games. No, he's not playing football, but he's also not sitting at home feeling sorry for himself. If there is an event where there is dancing, he dances, in his chair. And probably most importantly, he still has hopes and dreams for his future. He's choosing to live his life in spite of an accident that altered his life forever.

He and his parents have been my single greatest teachers, in regards to recovery and wellness. Early on, in observing him, his attitude, his perseverance, I realized that I had just been surviving in my own recovery. I wasn't thriving. I was not choosing to live in spite of my disorder.

As I watched this young man with this severe brain injury and his parents, I began to realize that he was doing a lot more than just surviving. Initially, of course, he went through a period where all he was doing was relearning skills and learning new ways to look at life and new ways to do things. In a sense, at that time, he was just focused on survival. But when he got past that point, he started thriving. Of course, prior to the accident his life was so different than what he faces now in a life filled with many challenges and difficulties. However, he taught me by example that I needed to stop feeling sorry for myself. I had justified my "poor me" attitude because I experienced something painful and difficult. But Tait and his family showed me I needed to start living life again. I needed to choose to live!

With a mood disorder, my life had been interrupted. It had been full of pain and difficulties. There were seven years where I was very sad and constantly depressed about what had happened, and it felt like my life had been taken from me. And yet Tait was my inspiration to see that no matter what happens in life, you can get back up and you can live. You can choose to live and enjoy the life that you now have.

There are only a few interruptions in life that bring about such significant change, but those interruptions change your life forever. Those interruptions come as a surprise to us, but they're never a surprise to God. What we think is a surprise in our life, He has known all along. He also knows how He's going to redeem everything that came about because of that interruption. Our life has meaning and purpose no matter what, because of Him.

Discovering that you have a mood disorder or having difficulties because of a mood disorder, are one of those kinds of interruptions in your life. This is an interruption that causes pain. It's an interruption that interrupts other people's lives too, and affects them. With this interruption, there is a necessary grief process that comes along with it.

After you work through that grief of coming to terms with your diagnosis along with the pain, havoc, and interruptions your disorder might have caused in your life, then it's time to get up, dust yourself off, and begin to move toward this new life that you have; choosing to live it. Please note, it's extremely important to fully work through your grief, and then it's time to move on with life. You don't want to get stuck in grief. You want to work through it. Your life may be a very different life than what you thought it was going to be; just like how Tait's life changed. He didn't think he'd be living his life in a wheelchair; he planned to be playing football. It's a very different life for him and for his parents. So, you grieve your old life, and you live your new life in spite of the grief and despite your circumstances. (And yes, everyone I know has some type of "circumstances.")

If you get stuck in that interruption of life and you don't work through the grief, you will end up being filled with self-pity, resentment, and bitterness. In fact, I think when you get stuck in the grief it's possible to become filled with what I call "toxic remorse." Every day that you're "stuck" in the grief and toxic remorse, you are missing one day of living. You will live your life in the past and you'll keep judging your future based upon your past. As we've discussed, that's not how to go about recovering in a positive, successful way. Don't let negative and toxic thoughts push their way into your thinking.

Will Rogers is often quoted as saying, "Don't let yesterday use up too much of today." You can't look in the rear view mirror and expect to move ahead. Instead, you and I have to choose to get up and move forward.

What is "toxic remorse," and why is it not good for successful recovery?

_____

_____

_____

_____

_____

Do you view yourself as a victim, or as a victor?

_____

_____

_____

_____

Who in your life is your inspiration?

_____

_____

_____

_____

Section 2

Surviving or Thriving?

In my training as a certified peer specialist for the state of Nebraska, I came to recognize that it's extremely important to understand the concept of moving toward something versus moving away from something. I had spent the first seven years of recovery moving away from my problem, wishing it wasn't there; I was focused on the problem, trying to survive my life. And suddenly, Tait helped me see how important it was to move toward my life and to live it.

There's a loss – a loss of the life that you thought you would have. But there's also gain. There are significant things that I've gained because of having gone through the pain of being diagnosed with a mood disorder and all the things I've experienced because of it. It's been said that for everything you have lost, you have gained something else. And for everything you gain, you lose something else. In these circumstances, you can either regret or rejoice. You can either become better or bitter. Again, it's a choice. And I began to clearly understand it was a choice I needed to make in spite of how I was feeling. We will be blessed when we "look forward with hope, not backward with regret." (Unknown source)

There's no doubt that an untreated mental health issue (or even after being diagnosed with a mental health issue such as a mood disorder) can bring about a lot of change into one's life. Lives are interrupted, and pain is inflicted. Relationships are lost or damaged. Loss of people, jobs, money, things, reputation, and self-esteem are all possible. These losses cause grief. If you don't work through that grief, at some point, you end up seeing yourself as a victim, and you end up feeling very hopeless.

Feelings of hopelessness can lead you to hopeless thinking. Hopelessness leads you to see yourself as a victim, and you easily "become" your diagnosis. Thinking thoughts like, "This is who I am. This is what my life is now. This is all there is for me." Your life begins to be defined by your symptoms and seems to be lived around your disorder. Your disorder begins to determine what your life is going to be like. However, seeing yourself as a victim will only rob you of your life.

Mood disorders, by nature, expect you to focus on the symptoms of the disorder and your feelings, which in turn will leave you stuck in the quicksand of victimized thinking. Here are several examples:

- Why even try?
- I'm giving in.
- I'm going to let this disorder define my life.
- This is all there is.
- This is as good as it gets.
- I feel sorry for myself.
- Why have plans when they won't ever happen?
- This is reality, so I might as well accept that my life is over.
- Why can't my life be easier?
- Why did this have to happen to me?
- Why does everyone else have an easier life than me?
- I'll never get better.
- My illness/disorder can't be managed.
- They're never going to get these medicines right.
- God doesn't love me.
- Getting better depends only on me, and I'm failing at recovery.
- My life is harder than anyone else's life.
- I can't go on; I'll never make it through this.
- Death would be better than this.
- No one needs me.
- No one would miss me if I were gone.
- There is something wrong with me.
- I'm a bad person.

- I'm weak.
- I must have a character flaw.
- I don't have enough faith.
- No one understands me.
- No one understands my problems.

Thinking like a victim is survival-based. When you are the victim, there is no thriving; only surviving.

The Bible gives us an example of someone who fell into that victim mentality in I Kings chapters 18 and 19. There you see that Elijah had seen a great victory and had even seen God do incredible things. However, because of his fear he fell into a time of self-pity and hid in a cave. After God's miraculous victory on Mt. Carmel, Elijah went to a cave to hide (isolation). He whines and cries and feels alone.

He says, "Oh, I'm the only believer left! There are no other believers. I'm the only faithful one."

You can almost hear him saying, "Boo-hoo!"

And the Lord comes to him and cares for him. He says to Elijah, "Eat some food and rest."

This is exactly what my medical team prescribed that I do when I was hospitalized after my manic event/episode. They developed a recovery plan of healing, rest, and closure, not only for me, but for my family and for the entire church. They recommended that I return to church not as the pastor of the church, but rather, to begin the process of healing, for us all to understand mental health issues—and to bring closure. The district president of my church organization had traveled hundreds of miles to the hospital, and he agreed this plan was in the best interest of all.

But for reasons unknown or understood by me, leaders at the church I had been serving rejected what the hospital had proposed and the district leadership had endorsed. (I'm not laying blame. People do the best they can under circumstances they've never before dealt with.) But it was the deepest wound I have ever experienced. I felt alone, I was confused, and I was unable to work. Yet the leaders of the church, to which I had dedicated my life for the past ten years, felt that my coming back for any time of healing and closure would impede the growth of the church. So, I was not allowed to do what the hospital recommended. And as if the pain and difficulty my family and I were struggling through wasn't enough, I was then made to resign.

And just as with Elijah, the Lord came to us through people who started Community of Grace. They knew I needed a safe place to rest, eat, and have time to heal. They came to me and said, "We want you to be our pastor, but we don't want you to work until the doctor says you're ready. You take however long you need. And when you're ready, if God wants you somewhere else, or if you don't want to be our pastor, so be it. We've done what we're supposed to do." Their sole purpose was to provide a place and time for my family to rest and heal (our 'nap' time) and to be ministered to. And not only did they continue my salary, they gave me an 18% *increase* in pay.

God's amazing ability to offer grace to Elijah is what He did for me. Eighteen months later I became their pastor, and I continue to serve at this church that I could never repay for their loving care and support. Because of their great love and care I was able to heal and begin my life "again." I was able to see myself as an overcomer as opposed to viewing myself as a victim.

Interestingly enough, isn't this what many of us need when we're feeling down, or alone, or feeling like life's difficult? Sometimes a good nap is all we need. Some good rest and some food can do wonders for our energy and abilities. Having a safe place to heal and rest is so very important in the process of recovery and healing. (It's my prayer that you, too, have people in your life who are willing to "hang-in-there" with you; that you might be able to have enough time to truly "heal-up.")

Here's what we can learn from Elijah: If you see yourself as a victim, just as Elijah did even though he had experienced this incredible act of God – a mountaintop experience– you will completely miss the beauty and joy of life and what you have to offer. Your purpose and the experiences you have to share will be veiled with self-pity.

Rooted in feeling like a failure, a victim, and discouraged, is the breakdown of one's self-confidence. I'm absolutely convinced that persistent mental health issues, and chronic episodes with your mood disorder, break down your confidence. Without confidence, the will to live evaporates, along with the ability to choose to move forward and live life.

It's so important to understand this. Part of choosing to live is based in self-confidence. If you're not able to choose to live, then your self-confidence and self-esteem has been tarnished and needs to be built up. All of us have something to contribute. Your life is worth living. God says so: "For I know the plans I have for you," declares the LORD, "plans to prosper you and not to harm you, plans to give you hope and a future." (Jeremiah 29:11)

Another sign of falling victim to a mood disorder is allowing ourselves to be defined by the disorder. Early on in my recovery, I did just that. Everything I talked about always related back to bipolar disorder, related back to what happened to me, related to my feelings. I actually began to think that the best part of my life was over. I would say things like, "I lost everything." Well, that simply wasn't true! I hadn't lost everything. In fact, the most important things – my family and my loved ones – I had not lost. And yet, here I was, filled with self-pity, acting as though I was a victim, believing that I had lost everything and the best was behind me.

My therapist cautioned me at one point against allowing bipolar disorder to define me. At first, I didn't get what he was saying. I didn't understand it. But then I began to grasp the meaning of his warning, and especially as I watched Tait in his recovery. I began to understand that one cannot let something, even a major interruption such as a brain injury or a mental illness, define you.

171

It is important in your recovery to recognize the fact that you're going to have periods of grief. There's no doubt that once one has been diagnosed with a mental health issue, there is a sense of loss. These periods of grief will show up at different and various times as you deal with a mental health issue. Based upon my own experience, grief really comes in waves. It's as though you're standing at the edge of the ocean and all of these huge waves of feelings and emotions and sadness come at you. This grief usually comes about due to losses that have occurred because of our mental health condition. Unfortunately, working through your grief also takes work. While those emotional waves come at you, you not only have to endure, but also have to press into them so you can work through the pain and the sadness of losses that have occurred.

Please note: it is very easy to mistake grief for depression. Knowing that difference and whether you are grieving, or dealing with depression, is extremely important. It's something that you will want to talk through with your therapist or in your peer-to-peer support group.

With this awareness, I began to try to change how I looked at life and used this information to work on me. I began to take responsibility back instead of blaming my disorder or my circumstances on everyone else around me. And I must say, it was extremely empowering.

During that time of my recovery I realized that my brain was re-wiring, just like Tait's did during his recovery. My path of recovery didn't involve relearning to walk and talk, and I didn't make noises that sounded like a moose in heat, but in fact, it really was a time where I was relearning. My brain was re-patterning thoughts and how I looked at the world. Suddenly, I began to move out of being the victim. I began to say, "I'm not bipolar. I was diagnosed with bipolar disorder." There's a big difference.

I realized that I had to stop just "surviving." I've got children, I've got a beautiful wife – I need to choose to live my life. Surprisingly, not everything in my life was about bipolar anymore.

Here's what I discovered: That I am somebody who has bipolar disorder, but it doesn't define me. It's not the sum total of who I am. There's so much more to me than bipolar disorder. As actress Sally Field encourages, "Don't judge yourself through someone else's eyes."

Here are my self-defining statements:

- I'm a child of God.
- I'm a husband, and many times, I'm a good husband.
- I'm a father, and I love my kids. (I wasn't a terrible father prior to treatment, but I did have some episodes where I know I hurt my children and my wife. But God has redeemed those things too.)
- I'm a grandfather. They call me Papa. And if I do say so myself, I'm a darn good Papa.
- I'm a son, and I still have roles and responsibilities as a son to my parents.
- I'm a pastor. A lot of people love me, care about me, and look to me for spiritual guidance.
- I'm artistic.
- I'm musical. I can write and play music. I can sing.
- I'm gifted as a visionary leader.
- I'm not athletic. I hate exercise! But I enjoy social activities and going to the gym to hang out.
- I've struggled with weight all my life.
- I have very flat feet.

That might be more than you wanted to know about me. But I'm trying to help you see that I'm more than just the sum total of "bipolar disorder," and so are you.

Take some time now to write out your own self-defining statements. If you feel like it, even write a poem about yourself. This is an important step in regaining your confidence. You must be able to see the good about you and the God-given gifts, talents, abilities, and even shortcomings that you possess.

_____

_____

_____

_____

_____

_____

_____

_____

_____

_____

_____

_____

Take some time and consider these very important questions:

Do you believe it's possible for you to have a rich, full, meaningful life?

Do you believe that your life can be full of joy and hope in spite of your disorder?
> ... in spite of what you've gone through in your life?
> ... in spite of the pain?
> ... in spite of your present circumstances?

Do you believe you can live a rich, full, meaningful life that has hope and joy in it?

I hope that you can answer yes to these questions. If not, I hope that you will take the time to work through the pain and grief that you still feel. Allow your loved ones, trusted peers, your therapist, and, of course, Jesus to walk with you through the grief and work through it so that it may no longer hold you back from moving forward.

Section 3

The Role of Christ in Recovery

"In spite of" … what do I really mean by that? To me it means that you keep living your life, or that you begin to live it again. Recovery is really about taking back your life. Some things change, but you keep going, and you don't let it get you down. You don't let it rob you of the things that it hasn't yet stolen out of your life. And you begin to retrieve those things that it has stolen. If you don't choose to live, sooner or later, your disorder will steal your life and everything in it.

A mood disorder should be treated as any other disease. When you are diagnosed with a physical illness, you find a way to assimilate the symptoms and the required treatment into your life. It doesn't consume your life. If you were diagnosed as a diabetic, you would work with a doctor and determine what you need to do differently on a daily basis. You would check your blood sugar and adjust your diet but you wouldn't stop doing the things you love because of it. You wouldn't tell everyone you know that you are diabetic and use it as an excuse not to live your life.

A mood disorder is just a piece of your life.

Being hopeless and becoming a victim is all part of a lie that you and I all too easily buy into. It's a lie straight from the Enemy himself. That's his job, to lie, kill, steal, and destroy. So what better time to do it than when somebody's down and out from the pain of mental health issues? And then he begins to speak these simple little lies into your mind and into your life.

He says, "Oh, life isn't worth it anymore. It's over now. The best is behind you. You can't have joy, and you certainly can't have hope, because you're just going to continue to struggle with this." These are lies, my friend.

The truth is, joy is possible. Hope is possible. No matter how difficult your circumstances are, no matter what you've been through or where you've been, joy and hope are possible because of Christ! For those of us who are people of faith, our God can do all things. Nothing is impossible!

In Mark 9: 21, a father of a boy asked Jesus to help them "if He could." I love Jesus's response: "What do you mean, *if*? With God all things are possible." I don't know about you, but I don't believe that God has changed at all, and that's the God I believe in. A God Who makes all things possible! I believe that God is just as capable and able today as He ever has been.

My faith doesn't have to be eaten alive by my mental illness. In fact, I won't let it happen. In my faith **Hope is a choice** through the power of the Holy Spirit, and from my perspective –a faith-filled perspective – I know that joy and hope are possible in spite of how I feel. And part of all this is to actively CHOOSE faith again, in spite of my feelings and moods. I CHOOSE to believe by the power of His Holy Spirit in spite of what I see in the natural.

There are a lot of things in life other than mental health issues that can make you feel miserable and terrible, and can really cause life to shut down. I've always told people: "Faith in Christ, the living God, is not a feeling. It's a reality in spite of feelings or circumstances."

In other words, I don't base my faith upon how I feel and I can't base my faith upon my circumstances. Instead, I base my faith on the reality of what God's Word says, upon the reality of what God has done for me now and in the past, and how He's shown that He will never leave me or forsake me in all those things. So I choose to believe that joy is possible, and that hope is possible.

Having hope is a choice. Hope is a choice that is based upon the facts of God's Word and our belief in God's Word. Hope gives us life. Hope empowers us to overcome our circumstances and the choice to live because of Christ.

In spite of how I might feel, how difficult my circumstances might be, in spite of what I can see all around me, out of my faith, and because of my faith through the power of the Holy Spirit, I have hope. And that hope fills me with His joy.

So let's look at some truthful statements, versus how previously we looked at the victimized statements of the hopeless.

Power-filled, Faith-filled, Hope-filled Thoughts:

- With God, all things are possible.
- God is for me, so who can be against me?
- God will not leave me nor forsake me.
- God has not given up on me, and He will not give up on me.
- God can take my pain and redeem it, and make it work for my good and for the good of others.
- I can help others with the same issues that I've gone through, with the same things that I've felt. I can help others.
- God is the source of my hope.
- I don't look to my situation to give me hope.
- I will tell my situation to sit down and be quiet, and tell my difficulties to sit down and be quiet.
- I will tell my big problems and my big issues that they are nothing compared to how big my God is, and how able He is.
- God can and will and is redeeming my past.
- God loves me unconditionally. No matter what my circumstances, I can have peace and hope right in the midst of them.
- God never promised that I would not have difficulties, but instead He's promised to give me peace in the midst of my difficulties.
- I need to know the truth, because the truth sets me free.

- The truth gives me hope.
- Forgiveness and mercy and grace are God's gifts to me.
- Success is built upon my failures.

For me, Christ Jesus is the key to a successful recovery. Why? Well, just look at who you and I are in Christ according to the Word of God.

Which of these hope-filled, faith-filled truths is the most personal for you? Why?

_____

_____

_____

_____

_____

_____

_____

You are what God says you are,
You can do what the Lord says you can do!

Who I Am In Christ Jesus

- *I AM* - **Blessed Coming in and Blessed Going out** (Deuteronomy 28:6)
- *I AM* - **Kept in Safety Wherever I Go** (Psalm 91:11)

- *I AM* - **Redeemed from the Hand of the Enemy** (Psalm 107:2)
- *I AM* - **The Light of the World** (Matthew 5:14)
- *I AM* - **Valuable** (Matthew 10:31; Luke 12:24)
- *I AM* - **Free From All Bondage** (John 8:36)
- *I AM* - **Justified** (Romans 5:1)
- *I AM* - **Strong in the Lord and in the Power of His Might** (Ephesians 6:10)
- *I AM* - **Dead to Sin and Alive in Christ** (Romans 6:11)
- *I AM* - **A Child of God** (Romans 8:16)
- *I AM* - **An Heir of God and a Joint Heir with Jesus** (Romans 8:17)
- *I AM* - **More than a Conqueror** (Romans 8:37)
- *I AM* - **Being Transformed by the Renewing of My Mind** (Romans 12:2)
- *I AM* - **A Temple of the Holy Spirit** (1 Corinthians 3:16, 6:19)
- *I AM* - **Washed, Sanctified, Justified** (1 Corinthians 6:11)
- *I AM* - **Walking by Faith and Not by Sight** (2 Corinthians 5:7)
- *I AM* - **A New Creature** (2 Corinthians 5:17)
- *I AM* - **Taking Every Thought into Captivity** (2 Corinthians 10:5)
- *I AM* - **Redeemed from the Curse of the Law** (Galatians 3:13)
- *I AM* - **Blessed with Every Spiritual Blessing** (Ephesians 1:3)
- *I AM* - **Holy and Blameless** (Ephesians 1:4)
- *I AM* - **Alive with Christ** (Ephesians 2:5)
- *I AM* - **Saved by Grace Through Faith** (Ephesians 2:8)
- *I AM* - **God's Workmanship** (Ephesians 2:10)
- *I AM* - **A Dwelling for the Holy Spirit** (Ephesians 2:22)
- *I AM* - **An Imitator of Jesus** (Ephesians 5:1)
- *I AM* – **Strengthened by Christ** (Philippians 4:13)
- *I AM* - **Rescued** (Colossians 1:13)
- *I AM* - **Redeemed and Forgiven** (Colossians 1:14)
- *I AM* - **Living and Growing in Christ** (Colossians 2:7)
- *I AM* - **Not Alone** (Hebrews 13:5)
- *I AM* - **Partaker of His Divine Nature** (2 Peter 1:4)
- *I AM* - **Healed by His Stripes** (1 Peter 2:24)

How does God see you as Valuable (Matthew 10:31; Luke 12:24)?

_____

_____

_____

_____

How does God see you as a Temple of His Spirit (1 Corinthians 3:16; 6:19)?

_____

_____

_____

_____

How does God see you as Redeemed and Forgiven (Colossians 1:14)?

_____

_____

_____

_____

_____

Which of these truths are most meaningful to you at this time in your faith journey? Memorize key Scripture texts that support them.

_____

_____

_____

_____

_____

Section 4

Finding Hope

So how does hope happen? Besides just saying, "I'm going to choose hope," how does it happen? How does it come about?

First of all, you find hope when you see and hear other people's progress. Make sure that you are around positive people who are faith-filled and encouraging – not people who "suck the life out of you" or who are trying to survive with their own problems – but people who are overcoming them and are filled with faith.

Secondly, you would expect me as a pastor to say this, but knowing God's Word is like taking "hope caplets." It's hope medicine. It's faith medicine. You take it and at first you may not feel any different, and it may not change you immediately. But the Bible tells us that God's Word never returns void, and I believe that reading it – or listening to it or to Scripture songs – can fill you with hope.

Another way to find hope is simply surrendering yourself to believing "God gives hope." You can finally stop striving and know that you don't have to do it. But He'll do it. And He'll help you do the things that He needs you to do. He'll empower you to do them.

Other ways to become hope-filled again include:

Remembering that your worth is not found in what you do.

- You are not a "human doing." Your worthlessness, so to speak, isn't found in your failures. But you are His child. Your worth is in who He has made you to be, through Christ. And you're a human being that is loved by God, and that brings incredible hope.

Remember God loves you and has forgiven you.

- Depression has a way of making you and me feel extremely guilty—and of course, hopeless. Guilt and shame also play a major role in depression. It's really important with depression to remember there is no shame and no condemnation from God. There is nothing that can separate you from Him.

Remember God has never left you in the past.

- Just a little bit ago, I encouraged you to not look in the rear view mirror but to look forward. But periodically, you certainly need to check in the rear view mirror for the faithfulness of God, to view the things He's done in your life. Look back at your victories and remember those things. If you're holding onto the past looking at the bad things, let it go. Focus on those things that were victories and where God didn't let you down.

Replace your toxic thinking with the truth instead of buying into a lie.

- A lie will always hold you. Remember, lies usually like to be secrets of the things we don't tell. These are usually the really nasty untruths and the deceptions. And so as truth sets you free, truth usually is willing to be out in the light. We're only as sick as our secrets. And those secrets that we keep so often are rooted in those lies. So it's important to get them out. Get them out in the open. Talk about them. Identify them and get rid of them, and replace them with truth.

- Paul tells us to take captive our thinking in 2 Corinthians 10:5. This is the process of believing that which is in line with God's word. In other words, recognizing that you and I are in charge of our thoughts.

Understand that hope is not a feeling, but a choice and a belief.

- This is where I might differ from someone who doesn't approach recovery from a spiritual perspective. I believe that hope is not a feeling; meaning, I don't have to *feel* hopeful. I can simply *choose* to be hopeful. Hope, for me, is connected to faith. It's not what I'm going through and not what I can see at the end of the tunnel. It's simply that I'm going to trust God. Trust that God is good and that

His grace will be enough. Corrie ten Boom once said that when you're riding on a train going through a dark tunnel, just because you can't see the light at the end of the tunnel doesn't mean it's not there. You don't get upset, or get scared and mad, or jump off the train and throw your ticket away. Instead you trust the engineer that you will come out of the tunnel sooner or later into the light. That's what hope is. Hope is: I trust God. Period. I'll get through the tunnel. This too shall pass.

Spend time with people who have hope.

- I really believe hope is contagious. I've come to the conclusion that in groups, foul moods and negative thinking are extremely catching. So if that's true, then hope is also something you can catch. You become like those you hang around with, so I choose to hang around with positive people. I choose to spend time with people who are faith-filled. I choose to be with people who have hope, because it infects me.

Forgive yourself and let go of self-condemnation and the stigma of your past.

- Turn it all over to God and trust in His forgiveness and the peace that it will bring. Stop hating yourself for everything you aren't. Start loving yourself for everything you are. The best way to escape from the past is not to avoid or forget it, but to accept and forgive it. This popular Tweet says it well: "The past is where you learned the lesson. The future is where you apply the lesson. Don't give up in the middle."

- Ruminating and toxic remorse will change nothing. Instead, embrace the forgiveness and mercy of the Lord and ask Him to empower you to move forward. And then by the power of His Holy Spirit (again asking Him to empower you) move forward with thoughts and actions that flow from a life of His mercy, grace, and forgiveness. Break the toxic thinking, self-condemnation, and remorse of the past by spiritually feeding on who you are in Christ. Sooner or later the spiritual food will cause who you are in Christ to become stronger and stronger, and the "old you" who was dwarfed by your mood disorder will begin to take a back seat to who you are in Christ!

Who has God made you to be, in Christ?

_____

_____

_____

_____

_____

Who do you know that has "contagious hope" someone you can plan to spend time with? How do you know that person has hope?

_____

_____

_____

_____

_____

Section 5

God's Purpose for Pain

By now, you might be thinking, "Wait a minute. This guy doesn't get it. He doesn't get all the pain that I've had in my life. He doesn't get how difficult that it is. He doesn't get the fact that they can't get me on the right medicines, and I keep having difficulties with the mood disorder itself. He doesn't get how impossible my situation is."

You're never a failure until you quit

Well, my friend, first of all, let me tell you, I know pain. I've had a lot of it. I've had a lot of circum- stances and situations in my life where I could have easily sat down and said, "Well, this is it." And I could have stopped moving forward. It would have been so easy to do so, and in many cases, people wouldn't have blamed me if I would have.

The reality is, you're never a failure until you quit. You're never done unless you stop moving forward. The specifics of your situation are not necessary for me to know, because if the God of the Scriptures is your God, you have hope.

This is a little poem I came across years ago, which takes a humorous look at never giving up:

TWO FROGS IN CREAM
by T.C. Hamlet

Two frogs fell into a can of cream,
Or so I've heard it told;
The sides of the can were shiny & steep,
The cream was deep & cold.
"O, what's the use?" croaked Number One,
"'Tis fate; no help's around.

187

Goodbye, my friends! Goodbye, sad world!"
And weeping still, he drowned.

But Number Two, of sterner stuff,
Dog-paddled in surprise.
The while he wiped his creamy face
And dried his creamy eyes.
"I'll swim awhile, at least," he said-
Or so I've heard he said;
"It really wouldn't help the world
If one more frog were dead."

An hour or two he kicked & swam,
Not once he stopped to mutter,
But kicked & kicked & swam & kicked,
then hopped out. . .
via butter!

One of the most undeveloped teachings in the Christian church at large is the issue of pain. There are a lot of us who believe we're supposed to have lives without pain. Somehow we've gotten the idea that life should be easy, life should be simple, and life shouldn't have a lot of difficulties. Well, that's simply not true. Life is difficult. Life is hard. Everybody's got problems. *Everybody.* Even the people who look like they have no problems, have problems. Even the people who believe they have no problems, have problems.

Let's dive into our biblical understanding of pain. The simple biblical understanding of pain is that pain is inevitable. Remember, Jesus says in John 17:33 that we will have many troubles in this world, but that He has come to overcome them. Difficulties, trials, and tribulations in this life are inevitable. How we respond to them is up to us. The problems will never end. Life never gets so good that we don't have any problems.

Here's where the theology of pain comes in. Pain is actually an opportunity for God to do incredible things. Pain is a wonderful teacher. It helps break through to our inner core and helps us put things into perspective and really see the Lord.

No doubt, an untreated mood disorder can contribute to a lot of pain, and even during the treatment of that mood disorder, there can be a lot of pain. Recovery can be painful. But within all that pain is the Lord's redemption. He didn't promise that you wouldn't have pain. Everyone in this life experiences pain and doesn't leave this world without it. Why should you and I be any different? I would challenge you to begin to embrace pain as an opportunity for growing and changing.

Maybe it's my experience as a pastor, but I have seen people go through a lot of difficulties in their lives, in all kinds of situations and with all kinds of people. I've seen pain that's far worse than anything I've ever experienced with my mental health. Even with extremely painful situations, I've witnessed people overcome and keep moving forward.

But I've also seen people who have less pain, if you will, or their circumstances aren't nearly, from all appearances, as tragic as others. And yet they quit, and the pain doesn't end.

I've stood at the graves where people have taken their own lives, and still saw families with hope. I've seen situations where people have lost loved ones in tragic accidents and still have hope. I've watched a nephew – in the midst of what I would consider to be a very life-altering, life-changing, difficult, very painful situation – still have hope.

Everyone has pain. Everyone has issues. Even your doctor and your therapist have their issues. They have pain in their lives to deal with. When you allow yourself to fall victim to your disorder is when you begin to believe that your life is more painful than it should be, and somehow that pain has robbed you. Don't let it. Grow stronger from the pain. Don't let it destroy you.

Khalil Gibran says, "Pain is the breaking of the shell that encloses your understanding." To me, that says it all. God is in the business of taking our pain and redeeming it, renewing it, or renewing us through it, working it out for our good.

In what ways are you like frog Number 2 in T.C. Hamlet's poem?

_____

_____

_____

_____

_____

When is it a good thing to experience pain?

_____

_____

_____

_____

_____

Key Thoughts

- It's extremely important to fully work through the grief in coming to terms with your diagnosis, and then it's time to move on with life.
- You can't look in the rear view mirror and expect to move ahead. Instead, you and I have to choose to get up and move forward.
- When you view yourself as the victim, there is no thriving, only surviving.
- Recognize that you're going to have periods of grief in your recovery, and that you must work through them.
- You are not your diagnosis. It does not define who you are.
- No matter how difficult your circumstances are, no matter what you've been through or where you've been, joy and hope are possible because of Christ!
- Your worth is in who God made you to be, through Christ.
- Forgive yourself and let go of self-condemnation and the stigma of your past.
- You're never a failure until you quit.
- Life never gets so good that we don't have any problems.
- God is in the business of taking our pain and redeeming it, renewing it, or renewing us through it, working it out for our good.

Section 6

Making Tenet VI Personal

Consider what the words of Tenet VI mean to you personally. In the exercise below, rewrite Tenet V to reflect your own life situation. Be as specific as you can.

Fresh Hope Tenet VI

At times I have allowed myself to become a victim, "defined" by my disorder. Therefore I choose to overcome and live in hope and joy, in spite of my disorder.

John's Tenet VI

I have a diagnosis of bipolar disorder. This is my diagnosis, but is not all of me. I admit I go through times when bipolar is not a part of my life, but becomes my life. This is not who I am. I am a successful businessman, grandfather, musician, husband, son, artist, and follower of Christ. Therefore I choose to focus on my abilities and not on my inabilities. I choose to be joyful and to be a positive influence in my home and at work, and not allow my diagnosis to be my identity.

My Tenet VI

_____

_____

_____

_____

_____

Every time you read Tenet VI, take delight in how far you've come in your recovery and remember this day you have made the choice to live in hope and joy.

Q & A with the Psychiatrist

1. What are some treatment options to work through unresolved grief that I have in my life?

    Dr. Egger: All are variations of psychotherapy, either individual or group. Medications are not generally useful unless symptoms of medical depression are present. Asking the question, "What does the grief prevent me from doing or protect me from doing?" may help identify how it is functioning currently in your life.

2. How do I identify and overcome lies I have told myself about my identity, my self-worth, and my future?

    Dr. Egger: In the process of therapy these lies are identified by achieving and understanding that you are made in the image and likeness of God, and that the Gospel of Christ is the truth that sets you free of lies and distortions.

3. How do I know when pain is healthy and productive and something I need to go through versus something I am allowing to hold me back and hold me down?

    Dr. Egger: Answer these questions: How long have I been feeling the pain? What is its origin? What is it leading me to do in my life?

4.   What are the signs of healthy grief vs. signs of unhealthy/toxic grief?

Dr. Egger: Healthy grief is gradually realizing over a year or so that the last person or relationship still has meaning in the griever's life, but the meaning has altered with their departure. Signs of healthy grief include being able to put objects belonging to the departed away or to place in context with other objects of memory, avoiding real or emotional shrines to the departed, and the ability to form new relationships while understanding that they don't replace all aspects of the grieved relationship.

5.   How do Christians work through losses – so they make the most of their pain and not waste it?

Dr. Egger: By realizing grief and pain are healing processes. Each morning invite Christ's healing into the situation (I Peter 5:7, Philippians 4:6-8) and at the end of the day prayerfully search out the evidence of God's moving power during the day that is closing.

CHAPTER 7

Unlock Wellness

The Keys to Successful Recovery

Now that you have read through all of the Tenets of Fresh Hope and have a good understanding of them, I'd like to talk about the keys to successful recovery. Staying in recovery has been the hardest work that I have ever done. It's ongoing and it's difficult, but it's well worth it. This process has also helped me learn a lot about some common setbacks and typical hesitations that those with a mood disorder may experience while working through recovery.

Following are the keys of wellness I've come to understand. I share these with you so that you can hopefully avoid some of the stumbling blocks that I encountered when I first entered recovery. Each of these keys is also what we in Fresh Hope call a "Wellness Plan." In other words, each of the following is a key aspect that one must put into action in order to move into wellness.

1. **Connections**

   First of all, you're going to need connections. The right connections with the right people: Encouraging people, hopeful people, safe people, people with a positive outlook, people who truly love you and who truly care for you, people who are going to tell you the truth even though it may be hard to hear, people who will hold you accountable, people who are going to help you forgive your-self, people who are going to forgive you when you mess up.

Here are some of the connections that will be instrumental in your recovery:

- A Trusted Doctor – You've got to be able to tell your doctor everything and anything. The more they know, the more they can help you. The less they know, the less likely they will be able to help you.

- A Therapist – Someone you trust, one who is wise, and who helps you move forward. Not all therapists or all doctors are the same. They all have a bit of a different approach. You've got to find a therapist who works for you, one you feel safe with, but also who's going to challenge you to grow and step outside where you're at presently.

- A Support Group – People who are going through similar things are crucial. There will be people in that group who are farther down the line than you are and others who have just begun. I find that to be very powerful and very helpful. I believe peer support groups are one of the most helpful things in recovery.

- Old Friends – A friend or two who's known you for a long time, hopefully prior to mental health issues getting in the way of your life. They're going to tell you the truth with love. They're going to be there for you no matter what.

- New Friends – A friend or two who maybe are a few miles down the road in their recovery, who can encourage and help you know that it's going to be okay.

- Loved Ones – Our family and friends who we truly love and who love us. In recovery, many times we have a lot of relationships to mend and take care of. After that's done, some of those people are the most loyal people to help you. Your family, whether they like it or not, are part of your recovery. They need knowledge about your recovery. You can also help them learn about your recovery. In addition, you will need to give them permission to speak the truth to you in love, and you must agree that you won't become defensive or take offense to what they say.

- Social Interactions – Work in recovery is not all focused on the symptoms or the problems, but also relearning to have confidence being in social settings with people—and enjoying relationships.

2. Goals

The second key is that you need goals. You must have goals, something that you're moving towards. What do you want your life to look like? Are these realistic goals? As I learned in my Intentional Peer Support Training, moving toward something is by far more empowering than moving away from it. Those goals should be kept in front of you at all times so you can look to them, be motivated by them, and be motivated to achieve them. And when you reach your initial goals, you set new ones that will move you farther in your recovery. One of my first goals was to get myself in a routine, esp. a regular sleep schedule. After I settled into that habit, my next goal was to discover hobbies to occupy my time and give me fulfillment. Setting goals and then reaching them motivates you to progress in your recovery.

3. Knowledge

The third key is knowledge. You must actively learn about your disorder. Learning about mental health through your doctor or therapist is passive learning. They have a lot of information that they can provide and you can learn from. But actively learning about your own disorder – reading books, doing your own research, checking out blogs and websites – this is active learning. When searching the web, verify information to make sure it is credible. Subscribe to magazines such as "Bipolar Disorder" (BP Magazine) or "Esperanza," a magazine for those suffering from depression. Read and read and read. Talk to other people. Pick their brains. Find out from them what has worked. Knowledge will also be gleaned from your support group. It's important, as we do in Fresh Hope, to cover topics about life in general. Understanding your disorder helps you understand how it plays out in your own life and for others as well.

4. Faith

The next key is faith – confident that the Lord loves you, having a faith that's encouraging, uplifting, and is Gospel-oriented. It is faith in knowing that God hasn't left you and your coming to understand that a mental health issue is not a flaw in your character, nor is it a lack of faith. Do you belong to a church or do you have a place to worship? Do you have a faith-based community that you can lean on and learn from? Do you have access to the Bible and a spiritual mentor to really hear God's Word? These things can all help you put things into perspective. The original Fresh Hope group that I founded is based in our church, and many individuals who attend the group also worship with us each Sunday. It's a wonderful, loving place for recovery.

I have to be honest. I used to be one of those pastors who, when people would come in and say how depressed they were, I would just encourage them to pull up their spiritual bootstraps, read the Bible more, and be positive! Then, when I was at the depths of despair and suicide myself, I realized that there was a lot more to this depression than just following the advice I had always given, and that it was impossible for me to just "pull up my bootstraps."

Faith is the foundation. You must have faith and believe in God's power, and then apply everything else you know. "Sometimes God lets you hit rock bottom so that you will discover that He is the rock at the bottom."

5. Hope

The next key is hope. As the basis of this book, we have already covered this in detail, but as you enter recovery, there will be days and times when you feel hopeless and that having hope seems impossible. This is when you remember this point and pull out this book. You review Chapter Four and recite the following words over and over: "No matter how I feel today, I have hope." You do not have to have it all figured out to move forward. Here's a good acronym for HOPE: Hold On, Pain Ends.

6. Focus

Focus is another key of successful recovery. Or you might call it "persever-ance" or "tenacity," because recovery takes time, and it's a process. You will experience setbacks here and there. You're going to have medicine changes and situations that leave you frustrated and wanting to give up. There are going to be days that are better than others, and there are going to be some difficult days. Every now and then, you may revert to old habits and old ways of thinking, but don't quit. Don't give up. Focus on your goal(s) and keep moving forward. Persevere through the tough times and remember that tomorrow is a new day.

7. Self-Awareness

Another key to successful recovery is self-awareness. Many times when we are in our disorder we've learned to avoid being aware of our thoughts, feelings and behaviors, because too often, it's too painful or too difficult. We go about life and give in to our mood disorder. But recovery requires you and me to become aware of our behaviors and ourselves. You must pay attention to yourself, how you feel, what your thoughts are focused on, how you are acting, and what your schedule is like.

In the beginning of recovery, it is extremely helpful to keep a mood chart. This will give you information about your moods and allows you to pause and iden-tify potential triggers. Are you talking too much? Maybe not talking enough? How's your mood? What are your triggers? What sets you off? What can you do to be proactive about those triggers and how can you work through them so they don't trigger you as much, or at all? Are you making good choices?

Journaling can help you as well. Write about what you did each day. Write about your feelings. This will also help you see progress. After a few weeks or months, you'll look back at your journal entries and realize just how much things have changed and how much you've grown.

8. Honesty

Honesty is an extremely important part of recovery. In order to get better, you and I have to be truly honest with ourselves first and foremost. We've got to be honest with what we're really thinking and why we do what we do. As painful as it might be, we've got to be honest with how we've been in the past. Honesty includes completely opening up and telling things to the appropriate people and not holding anything back from them.

For instance, sometimes we like to tell our doctor one thing, and then fail to mention that detail to the therapist, but bring up something else to the therapist. All of our key connections involved with our care and recovery need to be informed of everything.

Being open, honest, and transparent especially with those who are helping you, and within a safe group such as Fresh Hope, can allow you to really begin to receive feedback about yourself. That feedback begins to help you change, and it helps you to see yourself more accurately. There are always those things that other people see in us that we don't see in ourselves, behaviors that we do need to know so we can grow and change.

9. Accountability

Accountability is really an extension of honesty, and I truly believe that if you want a successful recovery, it's imperative to have a circle of accountability.

As we previously discussed in Chapter 3, a circle of accountability involves placing yourself smack dab in the middle of a circle with a group of safe people around you. This would include people such as your doctor, therapist, pastor, a trusted friend or two, people with whom you feel safe, who care about you and want to see you get better. This circle may also include a peer from your support group or a peer that you've known along the way, and one or two loved ones. Keep the group at five, no more than six and no fewer than four, and include people from different aspects of your life. Allow those people to have access to your entire life, give them permission to give you feedback, and also connect them with each other so that they can speak to one another and share observations and progress.

It's important for these folks to have access to your doctor and for your doctor to have access to them, and the same way with your therapist. That might be scary, and it takes a lot of trust in order to do that, but it's so important. You and I have learned how to play the game, to a certain degree, and we can hide certain things from certain people. The more the people who love and care about us, who are safe and truly invested in our recovery, are involved and fully informed, the better off we are.

10. Attitude

You need attitude. Not just any attitude. You need some real 'tude'! A positive attitude, a positive outlook. You need to detox that brain and detox your thinking and get rid of the stinkin' thinkin', start to push forward and say, "I'm going to beat this. I'm going to overcome this. No matter what."

11. Laughter

Another key to successful recovery, I believe, is laughter. You've got to laugh. Laughter helps your physical health and your mental health. It gets oxygen into your cells, it increases your endorphins, and it helps your serotonin levels. Too often, depressed people find other depressed people to spend time with. Find people to be around who make you laugh and who will help you find humor again. This will help your recovery.

12. Sleep

Sleep might seem like something that isn't that important, but for someone with a mood disorder, a regular sleep schedule is imperative. It must be a schedule that you and your doctor have agreed upon that is best for you, one in which you don't sleep too much and you don't sleep too little. Even people without mood disorders will tell you how the lack of sleep affects their mood.

13. Medicine

Most likely, or in many cases, your doctor will have prescribed at least one medicine, possibly more, to help treat your mood disorder. Medication needs to be taken as prescribed. This must be followed according to your doctor's instructions. Medicine cannot be effective if it's taken off and on, hit and miss. If you're not compliant and not taking it as prescribed, then the doctor will not know whether or not the medicines are the right ones. Take them in the right amount at the right time, all the time. Let me say that again: Take the right amount at the right time, all the time.

As we've discussed, you might have to put up with some side effects initially, at least for the short term, while your body adjusts to the medicine. Sometimes the side effects are long-term, but trust me, even with these, it's worth it. That's where you need to determine, along with your doctor, if you can live with those and if they're worth it for you. And yes, sometimes medicine causes hunger, and that hunger, of course, causes weight gain. Just remember, the medicine is helping regulate your brain so that you can live your life and be well.

14. Exercise

This is not one of my personal strong suits, but it is vital to recovery. Exercise improves everyone's physical and mental health. Many studies show that people who exercise regularly benefit with a positive boost in mood and lower rate of depression. When you exercise, your body releases endorphins, chemicals that trigger a positive and energizing outlook on life.

Simply put, it's for everybody, including those of us with mood disorders. It's important. I think it's important for me to get outdoors. It can be as simple as taking a walk. Taking in sunlight if at all possible is extremely helpful to one's mental health. Fresh air helps, even in the wintertime. Now of course, exercise is extremely important if you've had any weight gain due to medicine, because it will help burn more calories. Join a gym, start exercising with a friend, or just to try to move a little bit more, starting with at least 10 minutes a day. This small step will make you feel so much better.

15. Diet

There are a number of medicines that are prescribed for mood disorders that cause weight gain, and that's all the more reason to watch your diet. It's not easy to do. It seems as though some medicines particularly cause an increase in specific cravings, such as for carbohydrates. Early in recovery it is important for you to accept that weight gain might be part of the process. However, if you know up front that this is a possibility, you can establish a plan to work through this side effect and set specific goals for weight management and controlling your diet. Low fat, low carb options will most likely be best for this purpose. Find a way to incorporate fruits and vegetables into your daily food intake, and limit the amount of sweets and high-fat foods. This will be difficult at first, because you may feel down about the process, and this could lead to eating unhealthy foods as a way to cope and deal with the stress. Believe me, I can relate to this! But you could ask someone close to help you to have healthy choices on hand so you can reach for a piece of fruit instead of a cupcake or cookie. Many resources can be found online that can help you make a plan for healthy eating. This link to WebMD specifically talks about diet suggestions for those with bipolar disorder: http://www.webmd.com/bipolar-disorder/guide/bipolar-diet-foods-to-avoid.

16. WRAP®

Another key to successful recovery is having a WRAP® (Wellness Recovery Action Plan®). This program helps you develop a plan of self-management skills that will help you move forward in your recovery. Go to their website, www.mentalhealthrecovery.com/wrap, to find trainings across the country and a variety of resources on how to build your WRAP®.

17. Giving

It's important to your recovery to give back, to give of yourself, to do things for others instead of just focusing on yourself. Sometimes when we continually focus only on ourselves, we get so inwardly focused that we can't see anything or anyone outside. Helping others helps us do just that, get outside of ourselves. Mood disorders demand our attention. They can be like spoiled little rotten monsters that demand more and more of us all the time. But when we focus on others, it helps our mood. We feel better. We feel better in regards to having helped someone else. It enables us to focus on them and their needs, as opposed to ourselves and our needs.

Giving of ourselves also helps us see that what we've been through has enriched our lives and brought a certain amount of empathy and ability to help others. This wouldn't be the case had we not gone through those things.

This list of keys for successful recovery may seem very overwhelming at this point. Truly you can't set out to do and accomplish them all in a short amount of time, and sometimes you have to start where you're able and work on a few things, one at a time, and add more as you can. A Wellness Checklist is included in Appendix B to help you track your progress.

It's very important in recovery to understand that you do what you can when you can. Yet you always have to push yourself just a little more than what you're comfortable with, because your mood disorder's going to tell you, "No, no, no, no, I'm not comfortable!" If you only do things you're comfortable with, you're probably going to end up just where you've always been. You can't keep doing the same things over and over, yet expect different results. What you put up with, you end up with. So it's important that you have just enough discomfort that it's getting you outside of your 'normal' behavior.

For whatever reason, it seems like so many times folks who are in recovery end up sabotaging their own recovery. I am not sure why. Among a host of reasons, I suspect one of the main reasons we easily end up sabotaging our own recovery is because it's hard work. And we either get lazy or feel like we're failing at it, so we just give up: creating some kind of issue that sabotages our total recovery. We may or may not even be conscious of the fact that we are doing it. And let's be honest, sometimes staying stuck in recovery is easier than the hard work of pushing through. Sometimes staying sick becomes our identity. I've heard it said that sometimes one does not choose to get better until the pain of staying sick is greater than the pain of recovery.

I also believe that we often lack self-confidence. Chronic mental health issues many times rob us of our self-confidence. And so we believe that we can't do something just because we don't have confidence that we can do it, so we go ahead and sabotage it before we naturally fail at, let alone attempt, it.

I do know this: for whatever reason you might find yourself sabotaging your own recovery, if you really want to get well, it's imperative that you come to terms with why you are sabotaging. For instance, recently I encountered a young person who was having one hospital stay after another. It was as though they were stuck in a revolving door that went in and out of the hospital over and over. After a brief discussion with this person, they told me that they felt safer in the hospital. Life outside of the hospital was more complex, had more conflicts, and was more difficult. But, because they were not willing to really face what was going on, this person was in fact sabotaging their own recovery. Getting honest about that fear has helped this person move forward in their own recovery.

Be aware of any self-sabotaging tendencies that you have. Identify them. Deal with them.

One important question I've asked myself many times in recovery is, "When is the last time I learned something new, or did something new, or thought something new?" That is always a good indicator to me if I am growing or staying stagnant. None of us will arrive at perfection. There are no perfect people, including those who don't have mood disorders. Recovery is not about perfection. Recovery is not about avoiding mistakes. Recovery is about overcoming the mood disorder – each day. In fact, every day has to be taken one day at a time, one step at a time. Keep putting one foot in front of the other, and you will develop your keys to success – or if you will, the tools for wellness – one by one, bit by bit. Then you simply keep moving.

One day you'll look back and say, "Wow! There has been so much accomplished! I've really made it a long way." All of us, until we take our dying breath, always have some way to go.

Many years ago I heard it asked, and I'm sure you have heard it too, how do you eat an elephant? The answer: take one bite at a time. Recovery can look like a huge elephant, and it will sit on your chest when you look at a list like this, especially if you're initially in recovery. How do you start? What do you do? Take one bite at a time. Pretty soon, those keys start unlocking all kinds of doors for you, and it all begins to fall into place. And suddenly, you'll find yourself filled with Fresh Hope.

Complete: If I don't have goals, _____

_____

_____

_____

_____

_____

_____

How is faith key to your recovery?

_____

_____

_____

_____

_____

_____

Why is it important to be honest with yourself and your accountability and support groups?

_____

_____

_____

_____

_____

_____

What kind of attitude is needed for recovery, and why?

_____

_____

_____

_____

_____

_____

Why is laughter a key to successful recovery?

_____

_____

_____

_____

Are you growing, or are you stagnant? Ask yourself, "When is the last time I learned something new, or did something new, or thought something new?"

_____

_____

_____

_____

_____

_____

Key Thoughts

- Recovery is ongoing and it's difficult, but it's well worth it.
- You must have goals, something that you're moving towards.
- You must actively learn about your disorder.
- A mental health issue is not a flaw in your character, nor is it a lack of faith.
- Persevere through the tough times, and remember that tomorrow is a new day.
- Take your medicine when it was prescribed, the time it was prescribed for, and in the way it was prescribed.
- Exercise, sunlight, and movement are proven to make you feel better.
- Giving of ourselves enables us to focus on others and their needs, and helps us take the focus off our problems and situations.
- In your recovery, do what you can when you can
- Be aware of and deal with any self-sabotaging tendencies in your own recovery.

CHAPTER 8

Help! I Love Someone Who Has a Mood Disorder

Section 1

Who is This Person?

Section 2

Steps to Support Your Loved One
"I Don't Need Medicine!"

Section 3

The Tenets Are For You, Too!

Section 4

What About Me?
There is Hope...Fresh Hope

Section 1

Who is This Person?

I f you're reading this chapter, then most likely you have found yourself on a journey that you did not sign up for, just as your loved one who has a mood disorder did not choose it either. It's a journey that requires your understanding, love, and participation.

If you are the loved one of someone who has recently been diagnosed with a mood disorder, you might be experiencing a lot of emotions and feelings right now. Some of them may even conflict with one another.

You might be experiencing confusion, thinking, "How can this be the same person I fell in love with?" Or "Why can't they change?" "Why can't they control how they see the world?" "Why can't they change their behavior?"

You might be fearful – fearful of what the future might hold, of what's going to happen next.

You might feel as though it's draining the life right out of you.

You might be experiencing anxiety and panic. You might even have had an anxiety or panic attack.

You might be feeling guilty for not knowing that your loved one had a mood disorder or mental health issue.

Maybe you're feeling guilty because you've been angry with them for their behaviors. You might be angry, especially if your loved one has suffered a major episode that has left you and your family damaged by their behavior.

Or the behavior, and what seems to be the lack of ability to change the behavior, has emotionally drained you and other members of your family.

You've been on a roller coaster ride, no doubt.

You might have experienced some shock – and may still feel shocked and over-whelmed, especially if your loved one was diagnosed after a suicide attempt. And you weren't even aware of the fact that there was really anything all that wrong.

You may feel just plain worn out. Maybe you're battle weary. You've been your loved one's sole care provider or giver. You're the one who's been listening and listening and listening, with no answers to give.

Maybe you feel a sense of relief. You might be thankful to know that what you've been experiencing with your loved one has a name, and it isn't him/her choosing to behave this way. Instead you're just thankful that it has a name and that something can be done about it.

No matter what the case is, please understand: This is not a choice your loved one has made. They, too, are on a journey that they didn't choose to take. Their frustrating

Separate your loved one's disorder from them as a person

behavior, inability to think differently, inability to function as they normally have, and their confused reasoning and sporadic out-of-control behavior are all symptomatic of a mood disorder.

I encourage you to begin to separate your loved one's disorder from them as a person. There are things that the mood disorder has caused your loved one to think or do.

More than anything, I want to promise you that there is hope. Mood disorders are treatable – very treatable. There's hope for a bright future, and hope for life as you once knew it. It might be a little different. But the person you fell in love with is certainly still there. And there's hope that they'll return fully. The Lord's plans for your lives far exceed the circumstances of your day. Hope means holding onto Jesus. Grace means Jesus is holding you, too!

I want to encourage you also to engage in your loved one's recovery. It's very important to their success. It's important to your relationship. Your loved one will do better in recovery if you engage in that recovery through your unconditional love, your encouragement, your knowledge of the disorder, and helping them understand it as well. Always—speak the truth, in love, to them.

When new folks attend Fresh Hope group meetings, many times the loved ones ask these questions: "How do I help?" "What do I do?" "What don't I do?" And they say: "It seems like nothing I do helps."

I want to address all of this. How do you help someone who has a mood disorder?

What are some of the feelings you experienced when your loved one was first diagnosed? Do those feelings still exist? If not, what made them go away?

_____

_____

_____

_____

_____

_____

"Stuffing" your feelings invariably leads to tension, anxiety, and an eventual blow-up. What steps can you be taking as a loved one to determine the best way and time to confront the behavior?

_____

_____

_____

_____

_____

_____

_____

_____

_____

_____

Section 2

Steps To Support Your Loved One

For families and friends, sometimes a mental health diagnosis can be just as hard for them to accept as for the person with the mood disorder. But it can also be a relief. Finally, you have a reason for the mood swings (or what you've been experiencing within your lives). And then treatment can begin.

It's important for people with a mental health diagnosis, particularly mood disorders, to be active in their own care. But your support, along with them being active in their own care, is really imperative. They need you to come alongside and encourage them. You can make a significant difference in your loved one's acceptance, remission from the symptomatic issues surrounding a mood disorder, and long-term recovery.

Here are some specific things you can do to help:

- First of all, learn about your loved one's mood disorder. Learn everything you can about it. Learn about its causes, its treatment. If you have children with this person, understand the genetics of it, because many of these issues are hereditary.

- Encourage them, secondly, to sign a waiver so that you can talk to their doctor and their doctor can talk to you. I encourage them to do this as a matter of accountability. One reason is because what we perceive to be reality comes from our brain. It comes from what we experience and how we perceive it, and how our brain functions. If your brain isn't working properly, your reality is going to be off. This is what has happened to your loved one, probably more times than you'd like to think about. Someone who has a mood disorder has a different version of reality. They go to see their doctor. They tell their doctor, "This is my reality," and for them, it is REAL. If you can participate by going to appointments with them – as mainly a listener or an advocate – you'll be better able to clarify your loved one's perceived reality. This can really help the doctor identify how to treat the disorder.

- Learn to recognize the warning signs of low moods and high moods, anxiety attacks, and panic attacks – whatever your loved one suffers with. Learn how those symptoms look within your loved one's life. And if you notice symptoms, talk together about them. Do it in a loving way. Don't place blame. Confrontation is sometimes necessary, but it is possible to speak the truth in love. Most of the time, speaking calmly and not yelling, blaming, or distorting the situation will lead to productive results.

One time, my wife shared with me that she was concerned about my mood, and I became defensive right away. "Why are you so concerned about my mood?" I asked. She responded, "Well, you seem really grouchy, and you just jumped at me right now." Many things were contributing to my mood. I had just had gall bladder surgery, I was having nosebleeds, and I'd broken my arm about three weeks before I had the gall bladder surgery. I was having to sleep in a recliner, and had been in it for weeks because I couldn't lay in bed with my arm. My nosebleeds were driving me crazy and we couldn't figure out the cause. So I said to her, "Look, I think any normal person without a mood disorder would feel crabby and irritable right now, but I hear you."

As my wife modeled, loving confrontation is sometimes necessary. It's important to say those types of things to your loved one. It helps them. And if you can approach it in a calm, yet direct, way so that your loved one won't feel the need to be defensive, it will help them even more.

Encourage your loved one to stick with treatment, to stick with recovery, to stay compliant with medication and sleep patterns. And if it doesn't seem to be working, especially the treatment they're receiving from their doctor, or if the side effects seem severe, then encourage your loved one to talk to their health care provider. If things don't get better, you may want to suggest that they get a second opinion. Sometimes doctors don't click with the patient. Sometimes doctors don't pick up on everything. Doctors are human beings just like you and me, and also there's a relationship that has to be built to develop a level of trust. I once heard a psychiatrist say that if you're being treated, for instance, for generalized depression, and you don't feel better in 30 days, you need to fire your doctor and get a new one. Obviously this is just one person's view, but it's important to realize that it is okay to get a second opinion. It is okay to check out what someone else thinks or sees and analyzes. A different doctor can bring a fresh perspective.

Work with your loved one to help them keep their doctor and their therapist appointments. This is a huge help especially if your loved one is newly diagnosed and just starting on medications. They might be sleepy or drowsy or just adjusting to the side effects. Help them navigate through the system in those early days. It might require more than simply holding their hand. But don't assume the responsibility for your loved one's recovery. Expect them to have an active role. And do understand that early on, the diagnosis itself is a big adjustment, along with the medication, and the change in thoughts, behaviors, and choices. You might have to make some phone calls or follow up on a few things. Remind them when to take their medicine - how to take it, when to take it, what it treats, and why it's important. Maybe that's not necessary in your situation, but in any case, do whatever you can *initially*. There will come a point when your loved one will need to take over those things themselves, and you'll have to back up and step out of the way and let them do that. Early on, though, when they're first put on medication, sometimes they're tired and kind of groggy, and especially if they experience some severe anxiety or depression, it becomes almost impossible for them to even get up to do basic things.

Please note: The use of alcohol and street drugs usually makes symptoms worse and more severe, and it can keep the medicine from working. Help your loved one understand this, and certainly don't engage in it with your loved one. Stay away from those things. There are some medicines that you would not ever drink with, and of course street drugs should be stayed away from, period.

Sometimes your loved one might feel like your concern is interfering, and they might get defensive. That can easily happen during a mood episode, whether it's depression or hypomania or mania. Please remember that their behavior toward you is not personal. It's not a rejection of you. It would happen with whoever was helping, because what they're speaking out of, or what's happening, is being caused by the mood disorder itself. It doesn't make it any less severe when those words come or when they get defensive and take it out on you. But hang in there, even when your feelings get hurt, or even when it hurts you. Your loved one needs your support.

There is a line, where if it hurts enough or things seem out of hand, that you have to find different ways to approach the situation, to get help for yourself and how to best help your loved one. Whatever you do, don't stuff it. Don't just stuff it down and just keep taking it. Deal with it appropriately. Handle it appropriately. Blowing up will not help. Blaming will make things worse. Yelling and returning hurtful words with more hurtful words will accelerate the situation. Be sure to pick the right time to talk to your loved one about the words and behavior that have hurt you. If they are in the middle of a manic or depressed episode, that is not the right time.

My wife always told me that I used to be like an 18-wheeled truck coming at her. When I wanted something and was focused on it, and I was in a manic mood or a hypo-manic mood, she said it was just easier to get out of the way and stand aside and let me through. Arguing with me took such immense energy. I've many times apologized for that, and I now understand how I was behaving. I see it. But it was important for her, even though she knew it was best to just accept the behavior at the time, to not just stuff it, because she could have become very resentful. Sometimes I'm sure she did resent it, and of course sometimes she was angry. Nobody's perfect. You can't always deal with these things perfectly because emotions can be very intense. But I encourage you to do everything you can to understand that it's the disorder you're dealing with, not your loved one. Try to set healthy boundaries and know that some moods will just need to pass, and then deal with the behavior at the appropriate time.

Issues that need to be dealt with should be brought up when the person is in a healthy state, when your loved one can really receive what's being said. It may be when they're recovering or have come down from a recent manic episode. When you have those moments where they are interacting with you and "present", and they really understand what you're saying, it's important to seize those moments. Don't overwhelm them with attacks, but identify how you have been hurt and what needs to change in their thinking or behavior. Use "I" phrases such as, "I feel a lot of fear when I see your mood beginning to sink. I fear that when you retreat into the bedroom all day that you might not be willing to push through. For me, it causes a lot of anxiety."

Although it will be difficult to accomplish, it's important to do things *with* your loved one rather than *for* them in their recovery process. Initially, as I mentioned, there may be times when you have to make phone calls and you take care of small things for them. But as soon as possible, encourage them to do it, and you can do it with them for support.

Do things with your loved one rather than for them

Consider using times when your loved one's mood is stable to discuss and develop safety plans, or encourage them to develop their WRAP® plan. These things could include credit cards, car keys, and banking privileges.

You may even consider having a Wellness Agreement with them. In other words, this is an agreement that they will do certain things to stay well and push toward wellness. Included in that may be how they are going to communicate with you about not feeling safe, and how important it is for you to know what's going on with them in regards to anything that may have to do with suicide or suicidal ideation (suicidal thoughts). If your loved one has felt suicidal or has made suicide attempts, this agreement should include how they will let you know so that you can help keep them safe.

If your loved one becomes violent or suicidal, please call 911 immediately. You also need to be quite aware of where you might take someone if they're feeling suicidal – which hospitals are the ones to go to? Sometimes hospitals and recovery centers have a mental health assessment center as opposed to a regular medical emergency room. That's probably a better place to go, because they're better equipped to address mental health issues rather than physical emergencies. Also, many police across the United States are being trained in handling mental health situations, where they learn the skills to go into someone's home and effectively transport the individual. Instead of handcuffing them, they're trained to handle this type of situation differently than transporting a criminal. Request an officer who is trained to handle this situation or request that they do this with dignity and an understanding of the mental health issue.

You can also develop a Treatment Contract. It's a written agreement of steps to take to help someone with a mood disorder. In the contract, the person with the mood disorder agrees to give you permission to carry out instructions for treatment. This happens if the mood disorder were to make it difficult for the person to take care of themselves. And both you and the person with the mood disorder would agree as to where, when, and how the instructions would be carried out. This especially is true when people have psychotic breaks or are suffering from psychosis, or may just be so debilitated by either a manic episode or a depressive episode that they're simply unable to function. The Harvard bipolar research program provides a downloadable treatment contract that you can print and fill out. I'd encourage you to do that or speak with an attorney or your doctor about these sorts of issues. Sometimes it's important to have a power of attorney so you can act on behalf of your loved one for their good, for what's best for them.

In any case, it's important for you to keep your own personal boundaries. Being a caregiver does mean that you're giving up some things within the relationship and you're laying aside some of your own needs. But you cannot lay aside all of your needs. You have to be able to hold your loved one accountable for hurtful things, for hurtful behavior, or if they're not holding up their agreements to be compliant with their medicine, treatment, etc.

Sometimes the person with the mood disorder simply needs to feel the effect of their choices, even though their choices may have been made due to their mood disorder, its incomplete treatment, or the medicine not yet completely working. Sometimes the best way that we learn is when we suffer consequences. Don't do all the work for them. This is their recovery. You can help them, and it's important to help them, but as much as you may want, you cannot do it for them.

Mood disorders are most likely a life-long condition, but with appropriate treatment, there is hope. They're very treatable in most cases, and your support can and will make a big difference. I would encourage you once again to develop a Wellness Plan as a family – what your loved one's going to do, and what you're going to do for the sake of their and your own wellness.

"I Don't Need Medicine!"

What do you do if your loved one wants to stop taking their medicine?

The best way to approach this is to start with simple things, like reminding them why they're taking the medicine, and to encourage them to first talk to their doctor or therapist, or with people in their support group. Help them understand that taking medicine is not a sign of weakness. People with all sorts of ongoing conditions (diabetes, heart problems, asthma, or whatever it might be) take medicine regularly, too. And we don't think differently of them. We don't think they're less than whole because they have to take medicine.

Many folks who are bipolar, for instance, come to this conclusion when they're feeling better. They might say, "I'm going to stop taking my medicine. I'm feeling better. There's nothing wrong with me anymore," or they don't like the fact that they're feeling emotionally bland and they want to go off their meds. Remember that mood disorders (and especially bipolar disorder) affect judgment. They could possibly be experiencing a mood episode even with the medicine, or it could just mean that the medicine isn't working the way it's supposed to.

Going off medicine or adjusting it without talking to their doctor can cause symptoms to return and things to spiral downward. So make sure you explain to your loved one that you hear them, that you understand what they're saying, and ask for them to agree that they're not going to change their medicine or change any of their protocol with their medicine until they talk with their doctor. Say to them, "I'll make sure to go to the doctor with you and explain what you've said to me so I can help the doctor understand the situation. I'll be able to affirm and confirm what you're saying. I know that this is how you feel. This is what I'm seeing too." Reassure them that you will figure it out together.

Remind your loved one of the experiences of others. In a peer support group such as in Fresh Hope, you are able to bring up this topic. Those who have already tried this can talk about what happened for them.

Your loved ones probably are going to complain about the medicine at first. Most people have some side effects that make them physically or emotionally uncomfortable. They might say things like, "I'm gaining weight. I feel bland. I feel down. I feel sleepy. I feel fatigued." When I first started taking Depakote for my mood disorder, my thumbs would begin thumping up and down if I had them on a table, like how a dog's leg moves when you scratch his belly. It was embarrassing! And I was hungry ALL the time. But everybody kept saying to me, "Symptoms usually are temporary. Hang in there. Hang in there. Hang in there. It's worth it." And those who encouraged me to 'hang in' there were right. It got a lot better. As my body adjusted to the medicine, the symptoms subsided.

Many times people with a mood disorder will gain weight because of their medicine, and that's when you can really come alongside of them and say, "Let's join a gym" or "Let's start taking walks together." Don't talk about the mood disorder during that time, but just talk about and enjoy life, or go walk the dog together. Getting that exercise really helps both of you.

It's not good for somebody to just stop taking some medicines. This can be very dangerous. Discontinuing medication or adjusting it must be done by a doctor and in the proper way. If your doctor is a good doctor, they're going to listen. They'll be able to weigh whether the side effects are severe enough and changes need to be made, or if the side effects are possibly something that they just need to put up with for a while. Many times, the long term benefits outweigh the temporary side effects. If side effects seem to outweigh the benefits, your health care provider can help you figure out what will work better. Tell your loved one: Talk to the doctor about it FIRST!

Don't ever hesitate – either you or your loved one – to call the doctor's office. That's what doctors are there for. That's why doctors are paid. They are there to provide service. If your loved one is experiencing side effects or wants to go off their medicine, and they don't have an appointment for another three weeks, don't wait three weeks. Call the doctor right away, and let them know what's going on and see what they have to say. Give them the ability to intervene. And again, always use the support group. Use your Fresh Hope meeting to talk about things like side effects in the open.

You may find that your loved one will suddenly say, "I don't agree with my treatment. I don't want to take this particular medicine. I don't think I have bipolar disorder." Or they might say, "I'm not depressed," or "I don't have anxiety," and similar statements. Again, encourage them to talk to the doctor about it. If they say, "I don't like my doctor" then proceed to get a second opinion. It's usually best not to argue, but to make sure that your loved one knows that you hear them, that you understand what they're saying, and that you understand what their reality is. If necessary, remind them that going off medicine or adjusting it without consulting the doctor can cause symptoms to return or things to get worse.

Stay connected with the health care provider, the doctor and the therapist. Maintain permission to speak with your loved one's care team and periodically attend appointments with your loved one. Initially, my wife accompanied me to my doctor appointments. Then came a point when I went alone to the appointments. But I would always make sure to ask her if there was anything she wanted me to bring up to the doctor. Did she have a question about anything or concerns about anything?

Remember that part of Fresh Hope is identifying how we can maneuver through recovery TOGETHER, and communicating about medication and treatment plans is something that should be accomplished with everyone involved. Stay the course with your loved one and make decisions together about any changes in their day-to-day care.

What do you see as your primary role and responsibilities in caring for your loved one?

_____

_____

_____

_____

_____

What steps can you take if your loved one wants to stop taking their medicine?

_____

_____

_____

_____

_____

_____

_____

_____

Section 3

The Tenets Are For You, Too

I'd like to talk with you briefly about the tenets of Fresh Hope. I clarify this in the introduction of the book, but I think it is good to discuss here again. The second half of each of the six tenets is geared toward you, the loved one. It's your tenet. And I want to encourage you to work through your own recovery also.

Mental health issues can be a lot like alcoholism is in a family. It affects everybody. An undiagnosed or untreated mental health illness will affect everybody, one way or the other. It will affect family, friends, and people in the workplace. It just does, because it has to do with our behavior and thinking, just like alcohol or drugs change behavior and thinking.

If you came to me as a pastor and said your husband or wife is an alcoholic, I would first encourage you to go to Al-Anon. Enduring and dealing with the side effects of alcoholism can cause stress, and living within that context is stressful. It can affect how you see things and how you feel. It certainly affects your emotional health.

The Tenets of Fresh Hope were developed for the person with the mood disorder, but each one also has a section for the loved one (second paragraph in each Tenet below). Take a moment and read through each and identify a few things that apply to you and how you have dealt with your loved one since they have been diagnosed.

Tenet I

My life is affected by a mood disorder and can become unmanageable and hopeless, especially if ignored or untreated. Therefore, I choose the help and support of others to overcome the struggles and find more joy in life.

My loved one's mood disorder has also left me feeling helpless and hopeless. Therefore, I choose the help of others in learning about the disorder and choosing healthy boundaries for myself.

Together, we have understanding. We remind each other of the Lord's love, and that He alone can do all things. He is the source of our hope, and in Him we can overcome all things.

"I can do everything through Him who gives me strength." Philippians 4:13 (NIV)

Tenet II

My mood disorder has also affected my relationships and the lives of those around me. Therefore, I choose to overcome for both my own good, and the good of those who love me.

I haven't always responded to my loved one's mood disorder in ways that were good for the relationship. Therefore, I choose to learn better ways to communicate with, support, and encourage my loved one.

Together, we commit to speaking the truth in love, healing broken relationships and viewing each other as the Lord views us.

"So let's pursue those things which bring peace and which are good for each other."
Romans 14:19 (God's Word Translation, 1995)

Tenet III

My disorder can become an excuse. Therefore, I choose to believe I can live a full and rich life in spite of my disorder. I choose the support of people who will urge me to "push through."

At times I don't understand my loved one and can allow them to either wallow in their excuses, or push them too hard. Therefore I choose to learn healthy, appropriate ways to contribute to my loved one's recovery.

Together we do better than trying on our own. We will hold one another accountable for learning, growing, and choosing to push through in hope.

"Therefore, encourage one another and build each other up." *1 Thessalonians 5:11 (NIV)*

Tenet IV

My disorder can lead me to feel hopeless. Therefore, I choose to believe, regardless of my feelings, that there is help and hope for my physical, emotional, psychological and spiritual well-being.

At times I also feel hopeless, letting my loved one's actions and recovery define my happiness. Therefore, I choose to live with healthy emotional boundaries, and choose my own joy despite the ups and downs of my loved one.

Together we remind each other that our hope and joy come from the Lord. He alone is able to fulfill our needs in every aspect of our lives.

"For I know the plans I have for you, declares the LORD, plans to prosper you and not to harm you, plans to give you hope and a future." *Jeremiah 29:11 (NIV)*

Tenet V

While medicine is a key component in my recovery, it is not the only answer. Therefore, I choose to explore new ways of thinking and acting in my relationships and daily living.

I too have been part of the cycle of dysfunctional living, either thinking I had all the answers or thinking the problem didn't belong to me. Therefore, I choose to submit myself to learning new behaviors and taking responsibility for my own healthy, balanced living.

Together we choose freedom over suffering, and joy in living through self-knowledge in action.

"We demolish arguments and every pretension that sets itself up against the knowledge of God and we take captive every thought to make it obedient to Christ." 2 *Corinthians 10:5*

Tenet VI

At times I have allowed myself to become a victim, "defined" by my disorder. Therefore I choose to overcome and live in hope and joy, in spite of my disorder.

At times, I have viewed myself as a victim of my loved one's behavior and disorder, causing resentment, anger, unforgiveness, or self-pity. Therefore, I choose to separate the disorder from the person I love, forgive and let go of the past, and live as a contributor to successful recovery.

Together, we share in each other's victories and celebrate the whole person.

For God has not given us a spirit of fear, but of power and love and a sound mind." *2 Timothy 1:7*

What things would you like to do differently after reading through the Tenets?

_____

_____

_____

_____

_____

_____

Having a relationship with somebody who has a mood disorder can be extremely hard and demanding. It can be challenging to find the time, the energy, and most importantly, the patience. So it's important to realize you can be supportive and yet still care for yourself. Remember this. You're not alone. Success stories can be heard over and over at a support group, proving that mood disorders don't have to ruin lives or ruin relationships or ruin families. At a Fresh Hope meeting, as a loved one you will also learn positive ways of taking care of yourself so that you can stay healthy and enjoy your life.

Section 4

What About ME?

Caring for and supporting someone who has a mood disorder can be exhausting and overwhelming. So much time is spent on your loved one's mood, medication, treatment plan, etc. that you may be wondering if anything will ever be about you, ever again. This is where you have to tune into your own well-being and recognize when you are being neglected. Give yourself some love, attention, and rest whenever you can.

Here are some ideas about how to implement your own self-care plan within a treatment and recovery plan for your loved one:

You need to take time out for yourself. Take a break where you don't have to think about, live, or breathe recovery 24/7. It's okay to share the care of your loved one with others. That way you're not responsible for every detail. A good way to do this is to use the folks who are in his or her circle of accountability. And again, if you haven't joined a support group, if you haven't been attending, for instance, Fresh Hope, start now. You're going to hear about experiences, hopes, and failures from other people who are going through what you're going through. You're going to gain insight, encouragement, and hope.

Sometimes those who are giving support end up taking a little medicine themselves. It's stressful, and that ongoing stress can deplete the serotonin level in your brain just as easily as any other difficult thing in life. It may be helpful for you to see a counselor or to see the same counselor as your loved one. The stress can be very overwhelming. I would encourage you to always attend a support group meeting, especially through the bulk of the recovery. If not a Fresh Hope group, do attend somewhere where the loved ones are able to talk to one another. Through the peer facilitating of the regular Fresh Hope group meeting, I have found many times that the loved ones are the ones who benefit so much when we break out into small groups. They really need to talk with and hear from one another to be encouraged, and to gain insight and ideas.

Create a list of people you can call for support that might be your own circle of support. Include people you might meet through support groups, so that when you do need insight or just need to talk, you're able to call them. Be sure to include your pastor in that circle of care and also in your loved one's circle of accountability. Your pastor can be of great support and encouragement to you both. And just like doctors, you may have to fire your pastor if he or she does not understand mental health issues. If that's the case, then you need a spiritual counselor who will understand those things.

Be sure to plan activities for yourself, where you can go out by yourself, or enjoy a night out with friends or family. See a movie. Set up a regular time to go to the gym or take a walk in the park and enjoy the day. Not everything has to be done with your loved one. They have to function, they need to learn how to do these things for themselves, and you also need to have your own space. Do something nice for yourself every day. Pray and ask for help when needed. Remember that you are human too, and that your health and well-being is just as important in the recovery process.

Finally, don't take on too much. It's not healthy for you. If you're at your limit, then you need to back up and say, "We've got to do this differently." And you cannot be at your limit all the time. You cannot be stressed to the max all the time, or you can end up having your own mental health issue with depression or anxiety. I've seen this happen with some folks. It does happen. So it's important for you to take care of yourself.

Always look for additional resources such as reading books, magazine articles, and blogs. Read online articles with caution, because the information is not always accurate. But there are lots of good, credible resources available. This is just another way to learn through the experiences of others and get ideas to implement.

If you really want to help your loved one, you're going to have to make sure to take care of yourself and your own needs. You can't help someone else if you yourself are falling apart.

There Is Hope…Fresh Hope

Here are some questions you might struggle with on a daily basis:

- Am I being protective and helpful, or am I being overprotective and enabling?
- Should I pay off credit card debts from a spending spree, or should that be his/her responsibility?
- Will my actions help or will my actions hurt?
- Do I have hope?
- Do I believe this is going to get better?
- Do I believe my loved one wants to get better?
- Do I believe his/her doctor is the right doctor?
- Is his/her therapist the right therapist?
- Do I trust my loved one?
- Who can support me while I support my loved one?

Thankfully, you will never have to question how much God loves you, or that He will provide you with the strength and courage to carry on. If you don't have one already, I would strongly encourage you to find a spiritual home where you will be cared for and encouraged. You need a place where someone will lovingly remind you that Jesus is for you, He's with you, and He's not going to leave you.

More than anything, know that there's hope. God is able. In the years that we've been doing Fresh Hope, I've seen situation after situation that seemed so hopeless be turned completely around within a short amount of time. With Jesus, everything is possible. He can work miracles. And when you find yourself worrying about your situation, I would encourage you to see that as a sign that you need to pray about it instead. Give your worries to Him. Cast your cares on Him. Don't tell God you have a big problem. Tell your problem you have a big God.

Today, a diagnosis of bipolar disorder, anxiety disorder, PTSD, or clinical depression is not nearly as hopeless as what it used to be or seemed to be. There are many new methods of treatment and many channels for recovery. There's lots of hope. There are times, when you least expect it, that there's a breakthrough. So just like I encourage those with mood disorders, I'm encouraging you to take it one step at a time, and know that God's going to provide everything you need for every one of those steps. And keep coming to Fresh Hope or another support group, because there you meet people who can hold you up, encourage you, run with you, celebrate with you, and cry with you. When you have a burden and you share it, it lightens the load. And when you have joy and you celebrate it with a friend, it multiplies the joy. You, too, need hope. We all need Fresh Hope.

Take it one step at a time

What specific actions will you take this week to take care of yourself?

_____

_____

_____

_____

_____

_____

What benefits can you receive from attending a Fresh Hope support meeting?

_____

_____

_____

_____

_____

_____

Key Thoughts

- Being the loved one of a person with a disorder means you're also on a journey that requires your understanding, love, and participation.
- Strive to separate your loved one's disorder from them as a person.
- It's important not to "stuff" your own feelings. Avoidance leads to anxiety, tension, and a potential explosive confrontation.
- Mental health issues affect everyone in the family.
- The Lord is the source of our hope, and in Him we can overcome all things.
- Take time out for yourself. You can't help someone else if you yourself are falling apart.
- More than anything, know that there is hope, through Christ.

Living a Full Life

(NOT "THE END")

Years ago, my mom was diagnosed with fibromyalgia. At that time, not too many people had ever heard of fibromyalgia, much less did we know how to pronounce it or what it meant. But one of the things I remember that my mom told me the doctor said was, "Don't worry, you won't die from this; rather, you'll die with it."

In some respects a mood disorder is the same. If you and I work at our recovery, and stay in and proactive in our recovery, we don't have to die from our mood disorder. Having said that, I want you to be aware that it is possible, even when you're doing everything within your ability, that your brain chemistry messes up and you may end up in the hospital. But I believe there are too many times when we end up in the hospital not because of the medicine or our brain chemistry changing, but because we're not being proactive in our own recovery. So, if you choose to engage yourself in recovery and hold yourself accountable to others, there's a greater chance you'll never die from it.

So I choose to see my bipolar disorder this way. I choose to look at it and say, "If I stay actively engaged in my day-to-day recovery, I'm not going to die from this. It will die with me." And I like to look at it this way: My mood disorder will die with me, and as a person of faith, I know that on the other side of death is life everlasting, and I'm not going to have bipolar disorder there.

So in the meantime, I keep going on living my life. Yes, living with bipolar disorder, but not letting the bipolar disorder consume me. I will not allow my disorder to steal any more life from me than it already has. And in fact, I'm busy taking back from it what it already stole from me. As I live my life in spite of the disorder, I'm not only taking back life, but life is becoming more and more rich and full all the time. And as I choose to trust the Lord, and choose hope, I begin to be filled with joy. Then I live a rich and full life. The hope we have in Christ isn't about expecting the best to happen every time, but knowing that whatever happens in life the Lord will work out together for our good! (Romans 8:28)

One of the greatest things that brings me joy in my life are my grandchildren. They say that grandchildren are God's reward to you for not having killed your own children during their puberty. There's some truth in that, I suspect. But because I've chosen to trust in the Lord, and I believe in Him, I have been able to have hope. I've been able to choose hope. I've been able to get past just surviving my mood disorder. I've been able to get past just coping with it. And instead, my life's become rich, and because of that, I have been able to enjoy my grandchildren like nothing I know of other than the Lord himself. They, along with my children, my wife, and my extended family, bring me great joy. And my friends bring me great joy. It amazes me how God has been such a good God to continually give second chances and new beginnings.

I want to challenge you to do the same. I want to challenge you to choose hope, like this tenet says, to really choose hope and not become a victim.

A major part of the work that you and I have to do in recovery, besides detoxing our thinking, changing our unhealthy habits, and being proactive, is to take back our lives from that "mood monster" we talked about in Tenet I.

So much of successful recovery has to do with where your focus is. Is your focus on the "mood monster"? Is your focus on the problem? As I noted earlier, are you moving away from your problems as opposed to moving toward your life? Are you focused on moving toward your goals?

Where you choose to put your focus will have a lot to do with how you think and whether or not you see yourself as a victim. We need to focus on what the Lord's doing, through us and in us, in spite of our circumstances, or because of our circumstances. We need to focus not on the mountain, but on the Mountain-Mover. I like to use a paraphrase from Ron Kenoly's song "Go Ahead" (©1996 Integrity's Hosanna! Music (Admin. by EMI Christian Music Publishing): We need to focus on the fact that we may be going through hell, but we will get through. When you're going through hell, by the way, never stop. And when you're catching hell, don't hold it.

Focus on the mountain mover: God

Now, lest you think that I'm only approaching this whole idea of hope simply because it's a faith issue, I want to share with you the definition of recovery from The Substance Abuse and Mental Health Services Administration (SAMSHA), and note that they're not approaching this from a faith perspective, but just a recovery perspective – and also note how many times they mention hope and the idea that recovery brings hope. They say:

"Recovery from mental and substance use disorders is a process of change through which individuals work to improve their own health and well-being. They live a self-directed life and strive to achieve their full potential. The guiding principles of recovery are:

- *Recovery is person-driven,*
- *Recovery occurs in many pathways,*
- *Recovery is holistic,*
- *Recovery is supported by peers and allies,*
- *Recovery is supported through relationships and social networks,*
- *Recovery is culturally based and influenced,*
- *Recovery is supported by addressing drama,*

- *Recovery involves individual, family and community strengths and responsibilities,*
- *Recovery is based on respect,*
- *And recovery emerges from hope."*

These are very important to understand.

I want to give you a working definition of recovery and remission, from a fresh hope perspective: **Recovery is the process of finding hope, purpose, and meaning for one's life.** Stated another way, recovery is experiencing a meaningful life, *in spite* of any chronic brain disorder, mental illness, or any kind of mood disorder. Part of this process is a restoration of self-esteem, identity and confidence, and obtaining a role in society and/or one's community. This process does not focus on symptom relief only, but instead casts a much wider spotlight on hope and the whole person, so that they may in fact experience positive self-esteem, identity, and attain a meaningful role in their society and community.

Notice in that definition (taken from SAMSA and melded with some of my own ideas) that the over-reaching message is that hope and restoration of a meaningful life are possible.

Is it the life that you thought you were going to have? No. Is it the life you wanted to have? Probably not. But sometimes what we wanted and what we thought aren't nearly as good as what God has allowed and given to us. *In spite* of serious mental illness, chronic brain disorder, disease or mental health issues – a good, rich, meaningful life really is possible.

Recovery is about wellness. It's about moving towards the life you want versus coping and surviving life as you are now. It's about wellness versus coping, thriving versus surviving, living a rich meaningful life versus a broken and pain-filled life. I know you've been through a lot of difficulties and pain. I know there's a lot of brokenness because of your mood disorder in your life. I know it's hard to have pain. I know it's hard to go through it. And if you are going through a lot of pain and you are feeling like you can hardly be hope-filled or hopeful, may I be so bold as to honestly share with you that my life has never been better?

I thank God for the pain that I've been through. I thank Him for the difficulties that I've had. Without them, I wouldn't know how sweet and beautiful the days are when there is no pain. Without the dark valleys, I would never know how beautiful the mountaintops really are.

And I have to be honest: I love my life, bipolar disorder and all. I wouldn't have chosen it to be this way, but I would have never believed this could actually be better than what I had experienced prior in life.

Would I rather not have bipolar disorder? Well, of course. But you and I don't usually get to make those choices. We don't get to pick the crosses that we bear. It's been said that there was a man who was allowed to go to heaven. He kept complaining about the cross he had to bear, and the Lord said, "Fine, come up. Pick a different cross to bear." And he looked at all those crosses, and he thought, "Oh, what will I choose? What will I choose?" And the man ended up choosing the very one that he had complained about.

Keep moving ahead no matter what

Now, I want to tell you this: Getting to this place in my life has not been easy. It's taken a long time to get to this point, years of recovery. It's been hard work and it's been a process. Sometimes while working through a process, you have setbacks and difficulties. Sometimes you move one step ahead and two steps back. The important thing is that you keep moving ahead no matter what. And you never quit. Your best stories will come from your struggles. The seeds of your successes are in the failures. Your praises will be birthed from your pains. Keep standing. I have never seen a storm last forever. Seasons change. Be encouraged!

Now while I plan to stay in sustained recovery the rest of my life, it's something that I take day by day, and I do not take it for granted. Yes, there could come a time when my brain chemistry is altered and knocks me off of my recovery foundation, if you will. However, I'm going to make sure it doesn't happen because I wasn't doing my part in working through my recovery.

By the way, never underestimate the power of your peer support group in your recovery. I've seen more hope happen in our Fresh Hope group meetings than anyplace else. Powerful things happen within a group. As we say in Tenet VI, we're going to hang around people who give hope. Never underestimate the power of what you say and what you share, and how it can help bring breakthrough for others, breakthrough that allows them for the first time to have hope in their lives. I asked one of the Omaha group participants to write her story, a story of promise and recovery that she found through Fresh Hope. That story is at the end of the book in Appendix C.

It's also a very powerful place to celebrate victories with other people, and to see others as more than just their mood disorder or their difficulties. Celebrating with and encouraging one another in a group is extremely important. There have been times in our Fresh Hope group meetings where, over the simplest thing, we have applauded for someone because we knew it was a huge step for them in their recovery. Someone else hearing your story and your journey of recovery can bring the hope to begin or to continue on their journey.

Learning to celebrate just the smallest things in our recovery can really help us succeed in our recovery. Too often we want to wait to celebrate until we reach the entire goal. But doing that can often leave one very frustrated, because sometimes it takes a long time to get to that final goal. And many times there are some very bumpy days and months within that period of waiting to achieve the final goal. When we experience those times of frustration, we feel like giving up – and many times we do!

I found in the early days of my recovery that it was extremely important to celebrate every little thing at that very time I achieved it. So when I had a good day and felt as though I was really making progress, I celebrated just that day. I also discovered how important it was to not give up if I had a bad day. It was important for me to view it as just one day of my recovery that didn't go so well. I would go to bed that night and start over the next day. I wouldn't let myself use it as an excuse for giving up or allowing myself to slip into depression. (A couple of bad days do not mean you have a bad life.) And then if the next day was good I would simply celebrate it. And by the end of the next day I honestly had forgotten that I had a bad day the day before. And pretty soon I started having more good days than bad, and more celebrations. As you celebrate progress, life begins to look up and gives you another reason to celebrate. And before you know it, you've reached a major goal, and it was a joy getting there!

One of the things we started to do within our Fresh Hope group meetings is to have Milestone Celebrations. Once every few months we take time for everyone in the group to celebrate some kind of little marker in their recovery. While we call it 'Milestones', it certainly does not always have to be a huge milestone. Sometimes it might be the simplest of things that we need to celebrate as though they're milestones, because a major milestone is always made up of a lot of smaller milestones.

At the celebrations, everyone receives a stone that says "HOPE" on it. Then everyone shares what they're celebrating about their recovery. Sometimes what is shared may be a very simple achievement, but what is said helps someone else make a breakthrough realization of their own. It's so powerful and empowering. We encourage them to write this on the back of their stone in permanent marker and to keep those stones together in a visible place where they can be seen daily. Just like the children of Israel who would set up altars where God had done miraculous things, the same would be true of these stones. When you're having a difficult day or feeling unsure if you can be hopeful, you look at those stones and you remember what you have to celebrate and what God has already done in your life. These evenings are so positive.

One of the ways I learned how to celebrate was to reward myself for pushing through. If I was actively working on my list of negative and ruminating thoughts, and I was doing pretty well with it that day, then I would allow myself to go do something fun.

And during that time I would simply have my own little "recovery party!"

Learning how to take things one day at a time or one step at a time is to learn how to celebrate each of those small steps on the journey. It helps you learn that the process is just as important to celebrate along the way as it is when you reach your destination. Writer and Public Speaker Asha Tyson encourages us with these words, "Your journey has molded you for your good. It has been exactly what it needed to be. Don't think that you've lost time. It took each and every situation you have encountered to bring you to the now. And now is right on time." Too often we are so excited to reach a goal that we fail to stop and enjoy the little steps of healing that it takes to get to the larger goals.

And by the way, I believe it is EXTREMELY important not to beat yourself up if you slip up or stumble on your journey. Just get back

In spite of your mental illness, you can have a rich and full life.

up. Ask yourself (and God) if there's something to be learned from it. Then learn it. And then move on. Telling yourself you are a failure or giving up at that point is only going to get you stuck and impede your recovery. The truth is, celebrating is fun. And one celebration leads you to see your improvement for that day. And a good "party" makes you want to have another…and another…and another!

Bottom line: A mood disorder can rob you of yourself and of who you are. But part of recovery is to regain your life and live it again. Ultimately, it's your life and how you live it is up to you, including your recovery. Don't give up just because you had a bad day. Get a good night's rest and begin again tomorrow. It's up to you. In spite of your mental illness, you can have a rich and full life. Don't yield to your disorder, but instead be in charge of it. See it as something outside of yourself. See it as a mood monster that can't define you and can't take over. In fact, you take life back from it. And suddenly you'll stop just coping and surviving, and you'll find yourself thriving. Author and Artist Mary Anne Radmacher writes, "Courage doesn't always roar; sometimes courage is the quiet voice at the end of the day saying, "I will try again tomorrow."

Why is the pain of recovery worth it?

_____

_____

_____

_____

How will you know when you're past coping and surviving, and have moved forward into thriving?

_____

_____

_____

_____

_____

Key Thoughts

- I will not allow my disorder to steal any more life from me than it already has.
- As I choose to trust the Lord, and choose hope, I begin to be filled with joy.
- Focus not on the mountain; instead, focus on the mountain mover: God.
- Choose hope and not become a victim.
- Recovery is the process of finding hope, purpose, and meaning for one's life.
- Recovery is about moving towards the life you want, versus coping and surviving life as you are now. It's about wellness versus coping, thriving versus surviving, living a rich meaningful life versus a broken and pain-filled life.
- Sometimes you move one step ahead and two steps back. The important thing is that you keep moving ahead no matter what. And never quit.
- God is working in your life. Celebrate your milestones, small ones and big ones, as you achieve progress in your recovery.
- The most determined part of your recovery is to regain your life and live it again.

Scripture for Reference

Look up and summarize what these Bible verses say about *YOU*:

John 1:12 _____

_____

_____

_____

_____

_____

John 15:15 _____

_____

_____

_____

1 Corinthians 6:17 ———————————————————

1 Corinthians 6:20 ———————————————————

1 Corinthians 12:27 _____

_____

_____

_____

_____

_____

Ephesians 1:5_____

_____

_____

_____

_____

_____

_____

Ephesians 3:12 _____

_____

_____

_____

_____

_____

_____

Romans 8:1-2 _____

_____

_____

_____

_____

_____

_____

Romans 8:28 _____

_____

_____

_____

_____

_____

Philippians 1:6 _____

_____

_____

_____

_____

_____

Philippians 4:13

2 Timothy 1:7

Hebrews 4:16 _____

_____

_____

_____

_____

_____

_____

1 John 1:9 _____

_____

_____

_____

_____

APPENDIX A

The "One Another" Commands in the Bible

- Mark 9:50 Salt is good; but if the salt becomes unsalty, with what will you make it salty again? Have salt in yourselves, and **be at peace with one another**.
- John 13:34 -35 A new commandment I give to you, that you **love one another**, even as I have loved you, that you also love one another. By this all men will know that you are My disciples, if you **have love for one another**.
- John 15:12 This is My commandment, that you love one another, just as I have loved you.
- Romans 12:10 **Be devoted to one another** in brotherly love; give preference to one another in honor.
- Romans 13:8 Owe nothing to anyone except to **love one another**; for he Who loves his neighbor has fulfilled the law.
- Romans 14:13 Therefore **let us not judge one another** anymore, but rather determine this – not to put an obstacle or a stumbling block in a brother's way.
- Romans 15:5 Now may the God Who gives perseverance and encouragement grant you to **be of the same mind with one another** according to Christ Jesus,
- Romans 15:7 Therefore, **accept one another**, just as Christ also accepted us to the glory of God.
- Romans 15:14 And concerning you, my brethren, I myself also am convinced that you yourselves are full of goodness, filled with all knowledge and able also to **admonish one another.**
- Galatians 5:13 For you were called to freedom, brethren; only do not turn your freedom into an opportunity for the flesh, but through love **serve one another.**

- Galatians 6:2 **Bear one another's burdens,** and thereby fulfill the law of Christ.
- Ephesians 4:2 With all humility and gentleness, with patience, **showing tolerance for one another in love,**
- Ephesians 4:32 **Be kind to one another**, tender-hearted, forgiving each other, just as God in Christ also has forgiven you.
- Ephesians 5:21 And **be subject to one another** in the fear of Christ.
- Philippians 2:3 Do nothing from selfishness or empty conceit, but with humility of mind **regard one another as more important** than yourselves.
- Colossians 3:9 **Do not lie to one another**.
- Colossians 3:13 **Bearing with one another, and forgiving each other**, whoever has a complaint against anyone; just as the Lord forgave you, so also should you.
- Colossians 3:16 Let the word of Christ richly dwell within you, with all wisdom **teaching and admonishing one another** with psalms and hymns and spiritual songs, singing with thankfulness in your hearts to God.
- 1 Thessalonians 5:11 Therefore **encourage one another** and build up one another, just as you also are doing.
- 1 Thessalonians 5:13b **Live in peace with one another**.
- Hebrews 3:13 But **encourage one another** day after day, as long as it is still called "Today," so that none of you will be hardened by the deceitfulness of sin.
- Hebrews 10:24 And let us consider how to **stimulate one another to love and good deeds**,
- James 4:11 **Do not speak against one another**, brethren.
- James 5:9 **Do not complain, brethren, against one another**, so that you yourselves may not be judged; behold, the Judge is standing right at the door.
- James 5:16 Therefore, **confess your sins to one another**, and **pray for one another** so that you may be healed. The effective prayer of a righteous man can accomplish much.

- 1 Peter 1:22 Since you have in obedience to the truth purified your souls for a sincere love of the brethren, **fervently love one another** from the heart.
- 1 Peter 4:8 Above all, **keep fervent in your love for one another**, because love covers a multitude of sins.
- 1 Peter 4:9 **Be hospitable to one another** without complaint.
- 1 Peter 4:10 As each one has received a special gift, employ it in **serving one another** as good stewards of the manifold grace of God.
- 1 John 3:11 For this is the message which you have heard from the beginning, that we should **love one another**.
- 1 John 3:23 This is His commandment, that we believe in the name of His Son Jesus Christ, and **love one another**, just as He commanded us.
- 1 John 4:7 Beloved, let us **love one another**, for love is from God; and everyone who loves is born of God and knows God.
- 1 John 4:11 Beloved, if God so loved us, we also ought to **love one another**.
- 1 John 4:12 No one has seen God at any time; if we **love one another**, God abides in us, and His love is perfected in us.

APPENDIX B

Wellness Checklist

Wellness/recovery is the process of taking back your life and being "actively proactive" [note: NOT passive] in working your wellness plan so that you achieve the optimum management of your moods. This then allows you to live a full and rich life.

A complete wellness plan would include the following (check those you have in place):

_____ a formal WRAP® plan

_____ a positive and encouraging peer to peer support group/s

_____ a variety of supportive and encouraging friends

_____ a doctor or nurse practitioner who listens to you and is someone you trust

_____ a therapist who helps you grow and improve

_____ medicine that is working for you

_____ a time with the Lord in worship and prayer

_____ a circle of accountability: friends and and/or family who have access to your doctor and your therapist

_____ activities/interests that fill-up your "bucket"

_____ work: paid or volunteer which takes the focus off yourself

_____ time spent with others in which you are giving to them

_____ the right amount of sleep

_____ exercise

_____ fun/social activities

_____ friends

APPENDIX C

A Personal Story of Fresh Hope

by Sarah

T his is my story of how God gave me hope and a future…a story of Fresh Hope. My journey to Fresh Hope started in 2002, after what I now call "the perfect storm." It was a series of events over three years that essentially triggered my genetic predisposition of depression. First, I was a victim of identity theft. Shortly after, I was in a car accident, which led to my still-constant struggle with chronic pain. All the while, I was trying to work thirty hours a week and be a fulltime college student. I was stressed and overwhelmed to say the least.

But then the most exciting thing in my life happened… I got engaged to be married to the love of my life! I insisted on planning my own wedding, which added even more stress. The wedding was beautiful, and I felt so blessed. But even with this perfect new life ahead, something still wasn't okay. I was not okay. The first time I told my husband there was something wrong, his exact words were "Maybe you just need to exercise." At this point I couldn't even will myself out of bed, let alone exercise! I felt weak, broken, and hopeless.

When I acknowledged that my symptoms of depression were so severe that I wasn't able to function in my everyday life, I went to see an internal medicine doctor. *(That was a big mistake. I needed to have gone to a mental health doctor.)* He sent me home with a prescription for Prozac… the classic "go-to" drug for mild depression. Not only was it difficult to understand the concept of what depression really meant, but to then acknowledge I might have it, was terrifying. The stigma was scary, and I had no idea how others would react if or when they found out. After the initial shock, however, it seemed simple enough. I took the medication, and I felt better. 'A new reality that was a "tough pill to swallow.'

Years went by, and I did just fine on my Prozac. I taught elementary art for a few years before we started a family. We were blessed with three sons in a span of 4 years, and although our lives were stressful, we were managing. During this time I was following my doctor's orders regarding my medication. Soon after my third son was born, though, something changed. I was on the highest dosage of Prozac, but I felt as if I was on no medication at all. Completely frustrated, I decided to wean myself off my meds without my doctor's approval. That was the worst thing I could have done.

I was spiraling downward quickly, and taking my marriage with me. In a moment of despair, I reached out to God for help in a way I had never done. Though I always believed in Him, somewhere I had strayed. And, despite how long it took me, it is equally amazing to know that He was there the whole time, patiently waiting.

Once I reached out to God, I wanted to believe that He would just "make it all better." I didn't really want to put in the work. But after months of being off medication and not seeing a doctor, my illness just got worse. My children didn't have the mom they deserved. Nor was I the wife or mom I wanted to be. That's when I finally returned to the same internal medicine doctor in hopes that a new medication might help me. He suggested a different mood stabilizer, but after about a month I knew something wasn't right. My negative symptoms—irritability, anger, and other depressive symptoms – had increased rather than decreased. Instead of taking me off the medication, it was increased, which led me to the scariest place I've ever been in my entire life. I knew God was there; but I couldn't feel Him… couldn't see Him. It was just too dark. I started the plan to take my own life.

I clearly remember the night I was lying on the bed with my 1 year old, rationalizing all the reasons it would be okay for me to go through with the plan. It would be an accident, a tragic story. Everyone would rally around my family in support. The boys would miss me, but they'd be okay. I'd see them again someday in heaven, believing that my God is a forgiving God. He would know how hopeless and broken I was, take me under His arms, and welcome me home. At first these thoughts were comforting, but then I had a reality check. I became terrified of myself, and what I was capable of doing.

I was so scared. I knew I needed professional help. I called a psychiatrist to see if anyone was available to talk with me immediately, and thankfully, there was. The therapist talked to me about my suicide plan/risk level, and whether I needed to be hospitalized. In that moment, just by telling him my plan, my suicidal risk significantly diminished. (Since I had told him, it could no longer be an accident.) In that moment God turned my life around

I started seeing a psychiatrist, and was diagnosed with Type 2 Bipolar Disorder. Working together with her, being completely open and honest about my feelings, helped me get back on the right track. Talk therapy and medication management are not a quick process, but were the most essential part of my recovery. My therapist suggested I find a mood disorder support group, and after searching online, I found Fresh Hope, "a network of *Christian* support groups for those who suffer from mood disorders and for those who love them." God gave me the courage to go that same night, and there, for the first time in a long while, I found hope… Fresh Hope

Pastor Brad Hoefs led the group. He, his wife, and many others in the group have been an incredible part of my healing. These people who started out as strangers, took me in with open arms, and changed my whole perspective on God's love and grace. Once I chose to allow them into my heart and accepted their support, I was able to find more joy in life, in spite of my disorder. They often remind me that with the Lord's love, we can overcome all things. I learned to not let my disorder become an excuse, or let it define who I am.

I specifically recall one night when my heart felt so heavy. I cried as I shared my fears of the illness ruining my marriage. As they talked with and encouraged me, I felt the weight lift from my heart, and it was replaced with the warm feeling of hope and God's love. They understood my feelings of hopelessness, because many of them had been there. Some were experiencing their loved ones go through it, which helped me understand how deeply my illness had affected those who love me. I had the responsibility to get better for them, and not just for myself. Within the support group, I learned more about mental health than I could ever learn from doctors or through my own independent research.

After learning of my art background, Pastor Brad asked if I would lead the group in an Art Therapy session. The session went really well, and I felt more alive than I had in a long time. How refreshing to be using my gifts again, to be doing what God has always meant for me to do. I was then asked to facilitate a weekly Art Therapy group, which has continued now for more than a year.

Facilitating the Art Therapy group is part of what we, at Fresh Hope, call a "Wellness Plan," part of reaching recovery and sustaining it. A wellness plan helps us hold ourselves accountable for our own mental health, and gives our loved ones a tool to help us do it as well. Some of the other things in my Wellness Plan include working with a good psychiatrist *(the proper kind of doctor)* and therapist that I trust, and taking my prescribed medication diligently. Other wellness tools include basic ways to keep my whole body healthy… a good sleeping schedule, eating healthy, and exercising. Sustained recovery is **not** simple, and it is **not** easy… by any means. But, I know now that I have a responsibility for my mental health, and can CHOOSE hope, even on the days I don't feel hopeful.

Fresh Hope gives those who feel alone, overwhelmed, fearful, and hopeless, a regular dose of community, focus, comfort, and hope through a spiritual lens. Maybe you saw some of your own story in mine, and you are hurting or suffering and don't know what to do. If you are not sure where to turn, and you know in your heart that something is not quite right, please seek out a local Fresh Hope group. If there isn't one in your area, ask God if it is His will for you to start your own group. Through my experience I have found that many, many people deal with the same things I struggle with, and that there *is* a way to thrive and love life again.

If you are a loved one of someone who struggles with a mood disorder, life can be very challenging and confusing. You need support, too. My husband has also felt very alone, tired, and frustrated through this journey. Fresh Hope has given us both the tools to make our way through.

Fresh Hope has given me a new way to look at my life. God continues to use this group to help me in my recovery, and more importantly, shows me His plans for my hope and future.

> *"For I know the plans I have for you. Plans to prosper you, and not to harm you, plans to give you hope and a future." Jeremiah 29:11 (NIV)*

**To start a Fresh Hope group,
go to www.FreshHope.us**

**Or contact us at
info@FreshHope.us**

402.763.9255

Follow us:

**Twitter:
https://twitter.com/freshhopeomaha**

**Facebook for Fresh Hope:
www.facebook.com/FreshHope.us**

**My personal Facebook page:
www.Facebook.com/BradHoefs**

This book may be purchased with special
group discounts at www.FreshHope.us.